The Book of the Holy Grail

Books by J.R. Ploughman

Illuminati Connection
19th Century Boot and Shoe Making
Grimoreum Verum
Sacred Magick of the Angels
Pagan Northumbrian Runes
Faerye Magick
Ye Stone Missal (Gargoyle Magick)
Dr. Fian's Spellbook
The Guild Book
Stone magick

Discordian Titles
Speculation of Spencer
Lost Treasure of Eris
Credo of Carnithius
Discordian Times
Erisian Gems

Forthcoming Titles
Forbidden Writings of the Illuminati
Illuminati Connection 2
Old Tradition Crafte
Varena and Her Cats

The Book of the Holy Grail

by Joseph of Arimathea, 54 AD

Original translation by Thomas Jefferson, 1787 AD
Retranslated by Henry Mercer, 1853 AD

Edited by J.R. Ploughman

with "Keys to the Quest" by J.R. Ploughman

PULPLESS.COM, INC.
10736 Jefferson Blvd., Suite 775
Culver City, CA 90230-4969, USA.
Voice & Fax: (500) 367-7353
Home Page: http://www.pulpless.com/
Business inquiries to info@pulpless.com
Editorial inquiries & submissions to
editors@pulpless.com

First Pulpless.Com™, Inc. Edition October, 1999.
Library of Congress Catalog Card Number: 99-65427
ISBN: 1-58445-165-3

Cover photography by Wolf Morgan Image & Design
© 1999 by Wolf Morgan
Book Design and Cover by CaliPer, Inc.

Editor's Acknowledgements.

I would like to thank James Manchester, my Grand Master, for his faith and guidance. My mother Pearl, a Grail Princess and my guiding light who gave me my lineage and bloodline. My inspirational friends such as Joel Radcliffe, publisher and bookbinder extrordinaire. Aaron Baughan, my lead guitarist and one of us. Bradley Arnold for his undying loyalty and faith. My sister Ronda for her opposite faith and it strengthening mine. Two new friends, Wolf Morgan for his undaunting work for this cause and our goals, and J. Neil Schulman, my newest friend who has the faith and determination which has driven me on to success. Finally I would like to thank my wife and Grail Princess, JenniferLynn Olivia (Moppet), who has inspired me through times of discontent and hardship. And a very special thanks to Herr Schmidt, for his observance of family tradition. Lastly, to my son, Ed; he knows why...

—J.R. Ploughman, July 11, 1999

I dedicate this work to my wife Moppet, and all other females who open their hearts and allow Yse to envelope them, with her divine grace and understanding of the chosen response...

—J.R. Ploughman

Table of Contents

[continued overleaf]

Keys to the Quest

by J.R. Ploughman

Patriarch, the Merovingian Gnostic Church,
Order of the Holy Grail,
and
Grand Master, the Strict Observance—
Knights Templar/Illuminati,
The United Orders of the American Rite

Introduction

My grandfather, General Hugh Mercer, said that Washington and Jefferson told him that by its virtue and character *The Book of the Holy Grail* may one day be the *Bible* of the American peoples.
—Henry Mercer, 1858

In 1982 the book *Holy Blood, Holy **Grail*** by Michael Baigent, Henry Lincoln, and Richard Leigh hit the bookstands with a vengeance causing controversy within the theological theatre and unrest amongst traditional churches. The book presented a single idea, which was greatly supported by both hard core evidence as well as conspiracy theory.

Plainly, the theme of the book was that Jeshua ben Jusef (Jesus) may not have died on the cross, and that the Christian religion, devoted to that idea, was thus a hoax.

It is plain to see that as we near the millennium, church attendance has fallen drastically and belief in biblical tenets is no longer common. The church as a whole has become a billion dollar a year industry complete with accountants, press agents, bankers and well groomed stars who preach from lavish television studios, and whose emphasis is on liberating the congregation from their money as opposed to liberating them from sin.

If we are to believe the information revealed for the first time in *Holy Blood, Holy Grail* (and we do for it is all as they have said), then the religion which has been taken so matter-of-factly, is a lie based upon a hoax. The social toll that organized religion has taken on society throughout history is well documented.

We are rapidly approaching the millennium, and now it is time for certain truths to be revealed. *Holy Blood, Holy Grail* was correct for the most part. It helped pave a new road to theological truth. It also made people aware of the Holy Grail, for the first time in centuries.

The Holy Grail has been hidden and well protected since Joseph of Arimathea wrote down the Grail doctrine as it was dictated to him by the Neutral Angels, Rheddae, France in 54AD. The doctrine has always been hidden. Waite called us 'the Hidden Church'. It's veils have only been able to be penetrated by those on the Quest who were/are, pure of heart. It was protected by the family of Jeshua ben Jusef (Jesus), from where we get the Grail Bloodline and protected by the Cathars at Montsegur, the Knights Templar, the old witches of Scotland in the 1500's and finally the Illuminati in America in 1776. Each of these groups has been the target of the church, not for what we do, but for the secret we hold. But the church could never reveal that aspect of their purpose, for it would alert seekers, who would in turn seek us out.

The Holy Grail is the single most important mystery of creation. Its doctrine holds the key to life and explains where we come from, why we are here, our purpose etc. It will also answer the question many distraught people ask after a needless death or unfortunate circumstance, 'why did God do that'. In simple terms it explains why and how people are as they are. It shows the reason why we have different races and what the strong points are of each race, and puts the racial question into a perspective, never before revealed. This allows for better understanding. It explains the purpose and pitfalls of reincarnation, which explains many aspects about people.

This holy book was translated into English in 1787 by Thomas Jefferson, who was a Grand Master, Strict Observance-Templar, or simply, Illuminati. It is the *only* true American religion. The teachings, doctrine, philosophy of the Grail were in fact planned for the Chosen land which is the United States of America. Ours is the Chosen language, and this fact is well illustrated by how the Divine Mathematics apply to our language, and support Grail doctrine. This was all planned during the pre-existence in the Celestial Realm.

This book will reveal the how and why of the Holy Grail which has been drawn from the Book of the Holy Grail. It is the introductory discourse which gives the seeker on the Quest their beginning. It is the basics of the theology which have been prepared by the Patriarch specifically for the seeker. The ideas expressed within these pages have never been made public before. But it is not new-age pop culture adhering to politically correct thought. It is simply the facts with no embellishment or opinion.

This book is a series of chapters which explain the Grail doctrine and give a basic idea of each part of the Grail plan, so the seeker can become oriented with the Quest, and be put on the right path.

Who We Are and Our Purpose

In 1787 our separate Orders merged into one body to be governed by a Grand Master and a High Council. This body is called The United Orders of the American Rite—1787.

The principal Order of this esoteric body is the Order of the Holy Grail, founded by Joseph of Arimathea in 54AD at Rheddae (Rennes le Château) France. This order exists in an unbroken lineage of succession from that time.

Its purpose is to preserve, protect and Quest for the Holy Grail. Within this order is the Merovingian Gnostic Church, which contains the Templar High Priesthood that performs the Grail Rites.

The protectorate of the Merovingian families and lineage is the Knights Templar–Strict Observance, whose esoteric system is contained in the Order of Illuminati, founded in 1776.

The primary teachings of the O.H.G. is contained in the Merovingian Bible which was translated by Thomas Jefferson, himself a Grand Master of the Strict Observance–Knights Templar. The Merovingian Bible, also called the Book of the Holy Grail contains the doctrine of the Hidden Church, i.e. Merovingian Gnostic Church.

This sacred text was imparted to Joseph of Arimathea by the Neutral Angels who have dominion over the Holy Grail. Its doctrine is critical to the Grail Quest as well as understanding the war between good and evil which is a critical part of the purpose of the Quest for the Holy Grail.

This lesson has been prepared in order to explain the basic concepts of the Order of the Holy Grail as well as its doctrine and teachings. It introduces the seeker of truth and knowledge to the basic fundamental principles which define us as a unique religion/culture. Currently there is a dissatisfaction with conventional religion. This decline in faith has been caused by the church's lack of answers to the ills which plague today's world, society and community.

The religious world view of North America is essentially based on puritanical Christian dogma. This religious approach lacks credibility in that it does not explain life, nor account for the ills of the world. Rather than give purpose, it implies guilt by denial of the natural. Conventional religion, teaches 'churchism' rather than 'spirituality'.

The Merovingian Gnostic Church teaches spirituality, and provides answers concerning life and death, God, Angels, life of Jeshua the Teacher (Jesus), the truth about the crucifixion, where we came from, and what our purpose here is.

The answers to these and other questions were written down as a book of wisdom in the year 54AD by Joseph of Arimathea, the natural father of Jeshua the Teacher. The Book of the Holy Grail or Merovingian Bible was spoken unto Joseph of Arimathea by the Neutral Angels who brought the Holy Grail to the Terrestrial Realm (earth), from the Celestial Realm.

This doctrine has never been made public, thus A.E. Waite's description of us as 'the Hidden Church of the Holy Grail'. There are many reasons throughout history for this Church to remain 'hidden'. Some of the reasons are: we are non-Christian, thus subject to heresy laws; we deny the crucifixion which challenges the doctrine of conventional Christianity; we believe that God (The Great Architect of the Universe) had a wife who was a Goddess named Yse, we believe in reincarnation as Jeshua the Teacher did, which is recorded in the Pistis Sophia, we believe in prophecy and Divine Dispensation among other things regarded as heretical. Most importantly, we believe in a Sacred and Divine Bloodline which was established when T.G.A.O.T.U. divided himself and created Yse. And this bloodline was made manifest through Joseph and Mary, who were both the natural parents of Jeshua the Teacher, as well as they who were imbued with the Spirit of T.G.A.O.T.U. and Yse.

Much has been written on the Holy Grail through the ages. The Holy Grail has been man's most elusive and sought after mystery. Only the Order of the Holy Grail, which is the sole custodian of the Book of the Holy Grail, being the sacred writings and teachings of Joseph of Arimathea, holds any legitimate Keys to the Quest.

Only when one has been given the Keys to the Quest, can one begin the journey of the Royal Quest. The following is an overview of the Grail doctrine based on the current edition of the Merovingian Bible (*Book of the Holy Grail*) as was translated from the Grail language by Thomas Jefferson in 1787. It will give an overview of the doctrine and beliefs of the Order's Priesthood.

Doctrine of the Holy Grail

The Book of the Holy Grail requires that the reader believe certain things, which at any given time may contradict what they have previously learned in a religious, philosophical, logical and social setting. Some of these beliefs include: The belief in Angels; that there is a God who has a wife who is a Goddess; that Jeshua the Teacher (Jesus the Christ) did not die by crucifixion, that he lived for mankind and gave us his Sacred Bloodline which can be traced to a Godly place called the Celestial Realm which existed before the creation of the Earth; that there is a war between the forces of Good and Evil, and the evil forces can only be fought through special chosen females who are pure and innocent and are as the Goddess Yse, and one above all can remove the Curse on the Grail family, and she will restore the Wasteland.

These ideas may seem difficult to accept at first glance, yet they are no more difficult to grasp than the various doctrines of the world's religions. Yet, when one examines the doctrine and studies the *Book of the Holy Grail,* there emerges a complete picture which illustrates the purpose and history of mankind, even going back to the Celestial Realm. Though this requires belief, there is also the mystery of the Divine Mathematics which are exclusive to the Order of the Holy Grail, which not only help explain the doctrine, but prove it by mathematics. In fact, the doctrine of the Holy Grail is the only religious doctrine in existence which is provable by mathematics.

The Book of the Holy Grail and its teachings have been kept closely guarded by the Grail Family and Grail Priesthood for almost 2,000 years. Its Divine Knowledge answers all questions regarding: God and Goddess; where we came from; the purpose of life; what is good and evil; what happens when we die; what the mind, spirit and soul are; the harmony of the 5 races; reincarnation; the true ways of male and female.

These and many more questions are answered in the Lesser Book of the Holy Grail. In the Greater Book of the Holy Grail, the Laws of Man, Nature and the Universe are diligently explained.

But what is this book, and where did it come from? That is the focus of this doctrine, and will show where the answer can be found. The Doctrine of the Holy Grail states that there was once a God, existing alone before creation. This God was all powerful, yet He existed in loneliness. He soon tired of this existence and decided to create a mate. He was made up of all the forces of Order and Chaos, and to create a mate, split himself in two. His creation was a lovely Goddess, and He called Her Yse (pron. Issa). Thus He became the God of Order and She the Goddess of Chaos, or in simpler terms logic and emotion.

She became overly emotional with Her newfound existence and felt immediate love for the God. He then kissed Her and Her response was the first response of love between a male and female in the Universe. It became known as the Chosen Response.

They became the Sacred Father and Divine Mother, when they had children. Soon the Sacred Father created a place for them to inhabit. This place is called the Celestial Realm, and the time period when this took place is called the Pre-Existence (using our idea of physical existence as a reference point).

The Celestial Realm was perfect, and all who inhabited it were immortal and infinite. But this life was soon to become stagnant as the Gods and Goddesses (the children of the First God and Goddess), became discontent with their perfection.

They required Balance within their lives, so they needed to experience Order and Chaos. So the Sacred Father called a meeting of all the Gods and Goddesses and proposed a plan.

Seeing as they all knew what it was like to live in [illegible]
and be immortal and infinite, they had to also learn what it
was like to experience being imperfect, mortal and finite, in
order to appreciate their perfection. Thus the Sacred Father
would create for them, a world where these things could be
experienced.

In the Celestial Realm all beings were either Gods or Goddesses. Each had a Divine Dispensation, being a specific Godly virtue. Some Gods and Goddesses were Lesser while others were Greater, still others were Major and others Minor in these Divine Dispensations. As well as this, they were divided into 5 Races, as we have on earth (the Terrestrial Realm). And each Race had its Divine Dispensation.

The Sacred Father consulted all His children in this decision. Two of his sons were made consultants during the council, as they disagreed with one another. Michael was in agreement with the Sacred Father while Adamas rebelled against the decision.

The Sacred Father became torn, as His sons opposed each other. But He knew it was for the best that he create the Terrestrial Realm where all could be recreated imperfect, mortal and finite.

The Sacred Father allowed His children to choose sides. There were those who followed Michael, who knew that this decision was good for all. The other children did not wish to leave their perfect world and they sided with Adamas, who is also called Lucifer.

He told both sides that He would choose Neutral Angels, and send them to the Terrestrial Realm with the gift of the Holy Grail. If those who were on the side of Michael would Quest for the Grail as well as guard and protect it the pattern of the Divine Plan would work out well to the advantage of all, and even the physical, mortal, finite life would be good. If those who sided with Adamas (Lucifer) hid the Grail from those who would Quest for it, life in the Terrestrial Realm, would be short and hard with many difficulties, and would end tragically, yet all would return to the Celestial Realm (without the knowledge of Balance) to Perfection. And the cycle would have to repeat itself again.

The Neutral Angels brought the Holy Grail to the Terrestrial Realm through Melchezedek, who created the First Priesthood on Earth. This Priesthood was created to guard, protect and preserve the Holy Grail.

The Melchezedek Priesthood became the High Priesthood of the Holy Grail, by Divine Dispensation granted unto Joseph of Arimathea, father of Jeshua the Teacher.

Here, the High Priesthood became the first priesthood to be enclosed within a family, that being: Joseph of Arimathea and his wife Mary, Jeshua the Teacher, Mary of Magdala and Mary of Bethany. The Romans wished to murder Jeshua the Teacher as his teachings would undermine their socio-political ideology. In fact their doctrine was manipulated by the Luciferians. Jeshua's twin brother Thomas, also called Simon of Cyrene, took his place and was crucified in his stead.

The First Family escaped the Holy Land (First Chosen Land), and went to France (Europe being the Second Chosen Land). They settled at Marseilles and then went to the Languedoc and settled at Rhedae (Rennes le Chateau). Here, the High Priesthood taught its doctrine to the Celtic peoples.

During this period, the son of Jeshua the Teacher (now called Joseph the Second) entrusted his son, Joseph the Younger to be the Third Grail Keeper. Joseph the Younger strayed from his duties and took as a lover, the daughter of a tavern keeper. Though she possessed the Chosen Response, he failed to have her Consecrated to the High Priesthood as a Princess, before their love was consummated.

Note:

It is now Grail Law that if a Grail man becomes intimate with any female who possesses the Chosen Response but who is not first properly Consecrated as a Grail Princess, she will be regarded a Princess Maiden, by union with the Grail man, and may be admitted for Consecration.

For his indiscretion, Joseph the Second placed a curse upon his son, that Joseph the Younger would have to devote all of his incarnations to the Quest without rest, and never know the love of a woman. Thus the legend of the Fisher King who was wounded in the genitals, and could neither breed (bring children into the Grail Bloodline), or die (as he was cursed to walk the Earth forever), was born. The only way for the curse to be broken was for she who was a Perfect Grail Princess, and the Spirit of Yse to meet him and fall so much in love with him as to reveal the Chosen Response when kissed.

Joseph the Elder (Arimathea), felt that this curse was too severe. He then created a Sacred Ritual which is called The Marriage of the Elements, to help break the curse. This Ritual is our foundation and most Sacred Ritual. Joseph the Elder did this knowing that his grandson would always be part of the Grail Priesthood, but never have a chance to know the love of a woman, or a chance to have the bargain of the Curse fulfilled (being that a Perfect Grail Princess would fall in love with him, and upon being kissed would reveal the Chosen Response, and restore his life and the Grail to the Earth, which would restore the wasteland).

The Marriage of the Elements ensured that one day his grandson would have to perform this ritual, and that perhaps there would be a chance that he would find the Sacred Grail Princess during this ritual and she would manifest the Chosen Response.

The curse on the Grail Family has persisted, and the

Luciferian Rebellion has grown in power and continues to make life on the Terrestrial Realm hellish with wars, famine, strife, disease and hate. The Quest for the Grail Princess has been of paramount importance for almost 2,000 years. For only She with the Chosen Response can restore the Wasteland and recapture the Holy Grail...

The Book of the Holy Grail was given to Joseph of Arimathea as the Sacred Doctrine of the Grail Bloodline and its High Priesthood. It was delivered to him by Neutral Angels after his son placed the curse on Joseph the Younger. The Neutral Angels appeared to Joseph and he wrote down their accounts which were to become the Sacred Doctrine of the Grail Bloodline and High Priesthood.

Within the accounts written in the *Book of the Holy Grail* is hidden the Divine Secret of the Holy Grail and She who is the Sacred Princess can unfold this secret.

The book states that in the Fullness of Times, being the end times, there will be signs of the evil which Lucifer, Lilith (the hairy night fiend) and the Triple Headed Hecate will bestow upon mankind. This evil will occur in the time of the Third Chosen Land (which is America), and the Chosen Language (American English), will contain the Keys of the Divine Mathematics of T.G.A.O.T.U.

The Divine Mathematics are the Key to the secrets and mysteries of the Holy Grail in the Fullness of Times. With these keys, one can find the Holy Grail and know the virtues and qualities of the Sacred Princess.

The agents of Lilith and Hecate will fight to re-word the Chosen Language and try to destroy it as well as demeaning the Sacred Words which describe the Perfect Princess. Though there is a Grail language, we believe that American English was the first language in the Celestial Realm. This is substantiated by the Divine mathematics which only apply to American English and certain key words which describe the Grail

Princess and reveal the Sacred Equations of the Holy Grail. By Divine Mathematics the truth of the Holy Grail can be proven and demonstrated.

The path of the Holy Grail takes the Consecrated Priest and Priestess through 3 Physical Degrees which illustrate the Priesthood. There are also 5 Spiritual Degrees which the High Priest and High Priestess experience which show them the level of Divinity they have reached regarding the Holy Grail. Above these are 5 more degrees called the Royal Degrees or Degrees of Perfection.

The Priesthood of the Holy Grail and its religious doctrine is unlike any other belief system. It allows one to escape the traps and guilt of puritanical dogma and its repression and suppression. It provides understanding, illumination, knowledge and wisdom. It explains who and what we are and who and what God/Goddess are. It reveals the Purpose of Life, in which each person plays an individual, yet important part. Its Doctrine frees one from the self imposed bonds of guilt and negative feelings created by puritanical religion. It provides freedom in life and freedom from religious tyranny. It defines and explains life, and gives life a purpose.

Beliefs and Creed of the Merovingian Templar Church

1—We believe in a Sacred God and a Divine Goddess, who represent Order and Chaos.

2—We believe that once we were Gods and Goddesses in the Celestial Realm and that we were here created perfect, infinite and immortal.

3—We believe that we were recreated upon Earth (the Terrestrial Realm) in order to experience being imperfect, finite and mortal, that we could learn Balance.

4—We believe that we will be reincarnated many times that we can learn and become illuminated in the Knowledge and Wisdom of the Holy Grail.

5—We believe that people have the choice to either serve Michael by Questing for the Holy Grail and to protect and guard it. Or, serve Lucifer and hide it. And we have free will in this choice.

6—We believe that the Quest for the Holy Grail is the purpose of life.

7—We believe that Jeshua the Teacher was not crucified, but had to LIVE for us, that there could be a Sacred Bloodline and High Priesthood.

8—We believe that the Quest for the Sacred Princess is the highest honor one can accept. And in finding her, the Wasteland will be restored and the Luciferian Rebellion overthrown.

9—We believe that America is the Chosen Land, and her pioneers and their descendants are the Chosen Peoples, and that American English is the Chosen Language.

10—We believe in Divine Dispensation through the Spiritual and Royal Degrees.

11—We believe in the Royal Marriage where a man and a woman are Sealed for all time and eternity. We do not believe in divorce or separation in the Royal Marriage.

12—We believe that True Balance is Order and Chaos, within the individual.

13—We believe that all Priestesses, High Priestesses and Princesses must be of 'Water' only and NOT Fire. And thus they should not have any fiery (aggressive) traits nor should they take "smoke and fire into their lungs" (as is the requirement stated in the Pistis Sophia and Book of the Holy Grail), and we translate this as smoking and aggressive attitude. And she who does take fire and smoke into her lungs is NOT of the Grail.

14—We believe in the fight between Good and Evil, and we reject the ways of Lucifer, Lilith the hairy night fiend, and the Triple Headed Hecate.

15—We believe that all Priestesses, High Priestesses and Princesses must be opposite to both Lilith and Hecate.

16—We believe in raising our children to be High Priests and High Priestesses and she who will become a Princess is cherished above all, as she is Sacred.

17—We believe that Divine Mathematics can show us the Path to Illumination and that here is Divine Truth as shown in the Chosen Language.

Society of the Holy Grail Lecture

This lecture is given occasionally to the public in order to present the Grail doctrine to them. It starts with the lecturer introducing him/herself and then asking a series of questions, being:

1— How many people here believe that they have an idea of what the Grail is?
2— How many people here are on a Quest for the Grail?
3— Who believes that the Grail is an object, such as the cup used at the last supper?
4— Who believes that the Grail is connected with Christianity?
5— Who believes it is a pagan mythological survival?
6—Who believes it is simply a new age concept of internal examination which applies individually, rather than collectively?

Now the lecturer presents the short version of the Recitation of the Lineage, which establishes the basic beliefs behind how, who, why where and when the Great Secret of the Holy Grail was kept and transferred from the beginning, up to us now. This is the short version of the Recitation of the Lineage read before the Grail rituals.

Recitation of the Lineage

This is our most important landmark and describes our lineage and right to the Grail. It also explains our religious viewpoint and shows how we recognize history and describes the Energy we make use of in our practices.

¶"For all of history there have been guardians and protectors of the Grail mysteries, secrets and the Grail itself. Even as

The Great Architect of the Universe imparted these mysteries to Adam (the first man), and imparted him first guardian of this Secret Doctrine as it contained all the mysteries of the Highest.

¶Seth, the son of Adam was the protector successor, who taught the mysteries to the chosen ones who became the Order of Melchezedek.

¶Seth passed the mysteries to Enoch, son of Jared who was the sixth son is descent from Adam. And T.G.A.O.T.U. appeared to him in a vision.

¶In the distance a mountain arose unto the heavens, and Enoch was taken to the top. There he saw a magnificent triangle of gold, where within the center was engraved The All Seeing Eye. Also engraved on the triangle were strange characters which he was strictly warned never to pronounce.

¶Presently he seemed to be lowered into the bowels of the Earth, through Nine Arches; in the Ninth or deepest Arch, he saw the same brilliant plate which was shown to him on the top of the mountain.

¶Enoch, being inspired by the Most High, and in commemoration of this wonderful vision, built a Temple under ground. This happened in that part of the world which was afterwards called the land of Canaan, and since known as the holy land.

¶Enoch, in imitation of what he had seen, caused a triangular plate of gold to be made, each side of which was a cubit long: In its center he engraved the All Seeing Eye, and around it he engraved the same ineffable characters which the Great Architect had shown him. And he placed it on a triangular pedestal of white marble, which he deposited in the Ninth Arch.

¶When Enoch's Temple was completed, he received the following command: "Make me a door of stone, and let there be a ring of iron therein, by which it may be occasionally be raised, and let it be placed over the opening Arch, that the sacred matters enclosed therein may be preserved from the universal destruction now impending". And he did so, and none but Enoch knew of this precious treasure.

¶And behold, the wickedness of mankind increased more, and the Great Architect threatened to destroy the whole world. Enoch, perceiving that the knowledge of the arts was likely to be lost in the general destruction, and being desirous of preserving the principles of the sciences, for the posterity of those whom God should be pleased to spare, he built two great pillars on the top of the mountain, the one of brass, to withstand water, the other of marble to withstand fire. And he engraved on the marble pillar, hieroglyphics signifying that there was a most precious treasure concealed in the Arches underground, which he had dedicated to God. And he engraved on the pillar of brass the principles of the liberal arts, particularly of Divine Mathematics.

¶The flood took place in the year of the world 1656BC and destroyed most of the superb monuments of antiquity. The marble pillar fell in the general destruction, but by Divine permission, the pillar of brass withstood the water, by which means the ancient state of the liberal arts, and particularly masonry, has been handed down to us.

¶To Moses, God communicated His Divine Law. He also gave him the true pronunciation of his Sacred Name, which He told Moses should be found by some of his descendants, engraved upon plates of gold.

¶Solomon, being the wisest of Princes, had fully, in remembrance of the promise of God to Moses, that some of his descendants in the Fullness of Times, should discover his Holy name, and his wisdom, inspired him to believe, that this could not be accomplished until he had erected and consecrated a Temple to the Great Architect of the Universe, in which he might deposit the 'precious treasure', the secrets of the Grail.

¶He chose a spot for this purpose, the most healthy in all of Jerusalem. In digging for a foundation they discovered the ruins of an ancient edifice, amongst which they discovered the ruins of an ancient edifice, amongst which they found a considerable quantity of treasure.

¶All the treasures were collected and carried to Solomon, who upon deliberation, concluded to them to be the ruins of some ancient temple erected before the flood, and possibly was dedicated to the service of idolatry, he therefore declined to build on that spot, and chose another place, where the temple was erected.

¶And the Temple of Solomon was built to house, protect and guard the Secrets of the Grail

¶And later, Melchezedek, highest of the High Priests inherited the line of succession from the first temple and formed his Priesthood as a Temple, to house and guard the Grail. And from this line of succession and custodianship of the Grail, it was passed to Jeshua ben Jusef (Jesus) who taught the first Gnostic wisdom to his followers. And he spread this Gnostic wisdom throughout the land, and it became an interference to the political control and government of the land. For he taught his disciples how to think and embrace the Gnosis to become individuals, and to recognize the purpose of life.

¶And Jeshua ben Jusef took two women with which to work the current of the Grail, and they were Mary of Magdala and Mary of Bethany.

¶And he was arrested by the Sanhedrin (the council of Jewish Elders). And according to historic record, this took place on the night of the passover. But, Judaic law forbade the Sanhedrin to meet at night, in private houses or outside the Temple jurisdiction. Yet the record shows that they did meet at night to bring him to Pilate, to acquire a sentence.

¶And he was sentenced to be crucified, yet, even in those

times Roman laws regarding crucifixion were very precise, in both the manner of crucifixion and the reasons for crucifixion.

¶And the church claims that he died upon the cross after a few hours, which is not possible, as a man could last two or three days on the cross before he died. And his legs were to be broken, but they were not, and to break the legs of one who is on the cross is to weaken the support which the body has by the legs. Thus the pressures of the body on the lungs cause suffocation.

¶And some say he was speared in the side, but in the fourth gospel it is stated that he was dead when the spear was thrust in him (John 19:33). It is also stated in the gospels that death occurred, 'right before his legs were to be broken'. These and other events suggest that Jeshua ben Jusef had the duty to 'enact' the prophesies of the coming Messiah, and that he structured his life to fit the prophesies.

¶When Jeshua thirsts and asks for water, he is given a sponge soaked in vinegar, this is 'written' to appear as if it is done to further his torture. In fact, if he was losing strength, a taste of vinegar would restore or stimulate him. Yet when he inhales the vinegar, he utters his final words and 'dies'.

¶Yet he did not die. For being both the son of man and God he could not die, for his purpose was to serve mankind with life, not death. But he had to appear dead to fulfill the prophesy extolled by John the Baptist, so that he might escape persecution through a faked death. For this was always the plan.

¶And instead of vinegar, the sponge held a drug, that when inhaled would knock him out. And then he would appear dead.

¶He could not be killed for he knew the Grail, and to harm one who is of the Grail is to be cursed by their actions. But, a plan could be devised to remove him from their people and land, as he was an obstacle. And to spare his life they would not be cursed. And a bargain was struck that the prophesy of the Messiah who would bring a message of peace, and be sacrificed for it, would come to pass. But the real secret would be kept hidden.

¶And there were those scribes who would have this secret known to the true Seeker. And when they wrote the gospels there was two accounts given, that the true Seeker would have to carefully examine the contradictions.

¶The Gospels say that Jeshua ben Jusef was crucified at Golgotha, 'the place of the skull', which is a barren skull shaped hill. Yet it was Jeshua ben Jusef's brother Simon of Cyrene who was crucified here by an act of self sacrifice to save his brother Jeshua. The other account shows that Jeshua ben Jusef was crucified in a garden which held a new and unused tomb. Both the garden and tomb were owned by Joseph of Arimathea, his father who was also the High Guardian of the Grail.

¶It is also taught that the crucifixion was a public event, with many witnesses. In Matthew, Mark and Luke the crucifixion is shown as being observed from a distance, suggesting it was a private execution. The rarity of a private execution on privately owned land was highly unusual, and very suspicious. A crucifixion of this type under these strange conditions, easily could have been a cleverly staged hoax. And it would have had to have the help and agreement from the highest political sources.

¶Roman law also forbade the burial of those who were crucified. Instead, the cadaver would be left on the cross to rot, and be guarded by soldiers so that the body could not be stolen by family and friends for burial. Yet Jeshua ben Jusef had a private tomb, and Pilate, who would have had to be part of this most secret plan, even if through a bribe, entrusted the body to Joseph of Arimathea. All quite against the procedure of Roman law at the time.

¶It was after this event that Jeshua's 'hidden church' split up and they went into the world to spread his teachings. They gathered followers and taught them the Secret Doctrine which allegorically taught the Grail mysteries. And from this, the pure of heart and worthy followers would discover their part in the 13 degrees of the Grail.

¶Jeshua ben Jusef, Mary of Magdala, Mary of Bethany, Joseph of Arimathea and his wife Mary went to France soon after the 'ressurection'. Here the family established itself as a High Priesthood among the Celts. And Jeshua, who was now known as Joseph II, had children by both Mary's, and they gathered followers of the Grail Priesthood to guard and protect their Sacred Bloodline, lest the powers who sought to execute him came upon him to do their evil unto him.

¶And Joseph II was married to Mary of Magdala and Mary of Bethany, who were both perfect Grail Princesses and as such, held the Grail within and without them.

¶And the Sacred Bloodline was established, yet Joseph II cursed his oldest son, Joseph III, for loving a girl who was not of the Priesthood. And thus the Curse on the Grail Family which has created the wasteland came into being. That Joseph III, would never be loved by any woman for all his incarnations until she who was a Perfect Princess kissed him and showed her desire and love for him through the Chosen Response.

¶And until this happens there will be strife, famine, wars, disease and such in the world and it will not see true peace. But, if the Perfect Princess should give the Fisher King (Joseph III) her love and desire and the Chosen Response, the curse on the Grail Family and the Earth will be lifted and the wasteland will be restored. And then, Joseph II can return to save mankind and fight the evil of Lilith.

¶The bloodline of Joseph II lives on today, well hidden and protected, that if the Fisher King should meet his Princess, all will be saved and earn their rightful reward in the Celestial

Realm. And Europe became the second Chosen Land, as the first had been soiled by evil.

¶And he and Joseph I spread the Grail Priesthood all over France and Britain and imparted certain elements of the mystery to the Celtic mystery schools. And they found tunnels in the earth which led them to a far off land with months of journey and hardship. And here in this land they met a strange dark haired warlike people. And Joseph II walked among them and taught them of the Grail. And this land was America, which he named as the third and final Chosen Land. And here he deposited metal plates, graven with the doctrine of the Grail.

¶And during the middle ages, a secret society was formally and outwardly established, which was first founded by Joseph II. And its purpose was to guard and protect the Grail. This took place in the year 1118 and was called The Order of the Poor Knights of Christ and the Temple of Solomon. Also called the Knights Templar.

¶The Knights Templar started with 9 poor knights dedicated to this cause. Each one held a key to the 9 Arches of the Temple, which held the keys to the Grail secret.

¶And the Knights Templar taught Gnostic Wisdom and protected the Grail as well as sought followers who were pure of heart who would embrace the Grail. The High Protectors of the Grail were/are the Pactio Secreta, a secret society with an unbroken lineage who are the protectors of the Grail since the time of the Order of Melchezedek, which is the Order of the Holy Grail.

¶And the Knights Templar taught the truth about the crucifixion and the Grail to their members and followers. And they opposed the church for their teaching of lies and political control over those who sought true religion and spirituality. And the Templars blackmailed the church for a great amount of money (to further their work), or they would expose the truth about Jeshua ben Jusef to the world. For he could not die for our sins, as we were born from Gods and Goddesses thus could not be born in sin, and as such, his death would only mean our destruction. But the church created a false religion to keep people from the truth, and they sought only money and political power and land, and sought the Grail to hide it.

¶And the Templars trampled the cross under foot, as a sign to determine who was a spy from the church, as a spy would not dare act in this manner. However, the Templars knew that the crucifixion was a necessary hoax to preserve the Grail and he who carried the bloodline of the Gods.

¶The Knights Templar soon grew rich and powerful and preserved the mysteries of the Grail, the one true religion, Divinely given by T.G.A.O.T.U.. They had their own churches and preceptories all over France, Britain and Germany and were quickly gaining power over the Holy Roman Church. They were about to reveal the secret to the known world, which would help create peace, equality and freedom for all classes of people, as this doctrine is the only doctrine which could/can topple the church. It would destroy the inquisition and destroy their terror and heresy laws. As only through this belief could there be change. For all sin, guilt, suppression and oppresion would be erased.

¶On Friday the 13th, 1307 King Phillippe (Philip the Fair) of France, had all the Templars in France arrested and their properties seized. By royal decree, the Knights Templar were disbanded.

¶Many of the Knights Templar from the preceptory at Bezu managed to escape to Scotland where they were hidden by the peoples of the Crafte, as they shared similar beliefs, philosophies, fears and goals. And they helped each other survive.

¶Robert the Bruce, King of Scotland gave his help to the Templars, as he wanted Scotland to return to its Celtic roots. After the last Templar Grand Master, Jaques de Molay was burned at the stake by order of the so-called holy inquisition, the Order fell apart. Robert the Bruce, himself a Scottish Templar wished to give Scotland its independence from church control and return Scotland to Celtic laws and religion. He was made Templar Grand Master, after Jaques de Molay.

¶278 years later, evil King James VI wanted to wipe the Templars and their Crafte out, in Scotland and devoted his time, energy and money to doing this, as Francis Stewart, Earl of Bothwell, was heir to the throne after him, and Francis was the Templar Grand Master, and had the same goals as Robert the Bruce. King James even had the bible bastardized and re-written to suit his own ends, and justify his murder and terror campaign.

¶After the failed efforts of King James, the Templars and the Crafte united in the Grail. They met in council and decided to find a new land where religious freedom would be law. The New World seemed a good place in which to establish a Grail colony, with freedom from church domination, suppression and oppression. Grail colonies were established in Nova Scotia in Canada and along the east coast of the USA. It was done for the Grail peoples, for this was the chosen land where Joseph II had visited and left sacred records engraved upon metal plates and buried for those of the Grail to find.

¶The Order of Melchezedek came through the lineage of Robert the Bruce, through Templar transmission. It was transmitted also by him to the Glendenonwyn branch of his family. This transmission was brought to America in 1742 by the son of Bishop Glendenning.

¶In 1776 the Ancient Illuminated Seers of Bavaria, founded by Adam Weishaupt took over as protectorate of the Knights Templar and the Crafte, and as the custodians of the Holy Grail in the Fifth Degree. They fought for the freedom of America as well as France and became the most powerful secret society in the world having great influence over the Masonic Lodges of most of the world. They also held the secrets of Strict Observance Templar Freemasonry as well as the Melchezedek Priesthood.

¶Sir Francis Bacon and his Baconians, the seekers of the true mystery religion also forsaw the New World as a potential haven for those of the Grail. Bacon, himself a Templar and High Priest of the Melchezedek Priesthood, thought on how to educate a New World for freedom from the domination of the holy Roman church.

¶He had access to the tunnels which join the continents and countries of the world. He sent people to America by way of these tunnels, and they had with them bronze, copper and gold plates which held the secrets of the True Religion which was taught by Jeshua ben Jusef.

¶And these plates were sealed in vaults, to be discovered when the land was sufficiently settled, and T.G.A.O.T.U. would choose Prophets and guide them through mysterious means to find and translate these plates.

¶On Sept. 13, 1845, James J. Strang was guided to find and translate plates. He was instructed to dig under a tree on the bank of the White River in Voree (Burlington) Wisconsin. He first found 3 rectangular plates which are commonly known. But, there were also found 2 plates which were round, under these, which were only to be shown to the secret High Priesthood also known as the Council of 13. Using the Urim And Thummim stones he was able to translate these plates which were engraved in Enochian and Hebrew. One plate described how to retain the Priesthood of Melchezedek, and how to organize the Order of Illuminati as the true form of transmission for the Priesthood. The other plate described the landmarks of the Priesthood.

¶On July 6, 1846, James J. Strang founded the outer Order of the Illuminati by these plates and the instructions which were given him by Templars. The outer Order of Illuminati was linked to the A.I.S.B. of 1776. The Order of Illuminati still operates today, by virtue of the archives keeper, Wingfield Watson. After the assassination of James J. Strang in 1856, the Order of Illuminati and its Priesthood reverted back to the A.I.S.B. where it has stayed ever since.

The above statement given in part is, as it is entitled, The Recitation of the Lineage. This shows how the Melchezedek Priesthood was preserved through the centuries. The following is an examination of the Holy Grail from the point of view of popular history and literature.

The Holy Grail in Literature

The Grail is 'One' particular thing, absolute and unto itself. It is a thing so important as to have been handed down through an impressive line of succession. Two of the most powerful and secret societies created solely to guard the Grail were the Cathars and the Knights Templar. And it is from these two schools that most of the Grail myths, legends and romances have survived.

We shall concentrate on the clues, keys and hints in 'Parcival', written by Wolfram Von Eschenbach. For Parcival gives us the most important clues and ritual initiation allegory of all the Grail romances. Interestingly enough, the popular hints of the Grail are associated with Jeshua ben Jusef and Joseph of Arimathea. But here the legends trail off and the Grail is not mentioned for another 1000 years in the romance writings.

So, the question that most Grail researchers and Questers ask is; Where was it during all of this time? Why was such an important secret supposedly buried for so long? And, finally, why did it surface when it did, which was at the peak of the crusades, when the Frankish kingdom of Jerusalem was at its apex? Exactly at the time the Templars were at their strongest and the Cathar 'heresies' threatened to displace the dogma and oppression of Rome!

The Grail myths and legends are linked to both early Christian and Pagan mythology, tradition and legends. It is thought provoking that the Druids who enjoyed a high position in both politics and religion, reigned at the time when the Grail allegedly disappeared from history. And their tradition was called Culdee, a mixture of early Christian and Pagan mythology, legend and religion.

Some early writers suggest that the Grail was the cup used

at the last supper. Likewise, in Pagan mythology the Grail is associated with the cauldron of death and rebirth, which resurrected dead warriors. In this part of the legend, the main hero is Bran who possessed a platter on which, 'whatever food one wished theron, was instantly obtained'.

These themes are repeated in all the Grail myths, i.e. 'that which is needed, is supplied by the Grail'. Also when Bran died, he was decapitated and his head was used as a sort of talisman. It was able to perform a variety of magickal functions. Again, this theme reoccurs in Celtic religious culture called by some anthropologists The Cult of the Severed Head.

Severed heads also played a part in Templar myth and legend. In this case a head was set on an altar and was consulted as an oracle. In fact the first account of a magickal severed head was that of John the Baptist. These heads could insure fertility of the land, prophesize and protect the land from attack. The Templars, in their veneration of heads, carved stone heads, to which were ascribed special powers.

The Holy Land fell in 1291, and between 1307 and 1324 the Templars dissolved and were made illegal. Then again the Grail legends seem to disappear until 1470 when they again appear in the writings of Sir Thomas Malory, in 'Le Morte d'Arthur'. Since this time the Grail has actively remained with us, in pursuit and examination of the Quest.

Even during the Second World War the Nazis were active in trying to find the Grail and financed many expeditions to France to try and locate it. But this later Grail of Malory became the cup used at the last supper. In fact, the concept of this labeling of the Grail is the latest Grail concept, which has caused much misinformation and disinformation to be published and speculated upon.

There are certain Grail myths which suggest that the Grail was brought to Glastonbury by Joseph of Arimathea. Other accounts suggest that Mary of Magdala brought it to Marseilles, where her relics are still venerated. These early accounts suggest that Mary brought the Grail to France, yet they do not mention a cup or chalice. The association of a cup or chalice being the Grail, is strictly a concept of Malory and represents the later development of the legend, but, it is a true allegory.

Parcival holds some interesting keys such as the hero of the story, Parcival, being the son of a 'widow lady'. The widow's son plays an important part in both Gnostic and Masonic teachings. In Parcival's travels, he meets the mysterious Fisher King. This character is also be associated with the Cursed Son of Jeshua ben Jusef. When Parcival meets the Fisher King, he is given sanctuary for the night. While he is there, the Grail appears. But it is not suggested that the Grail is associated with Jeshua ben Jusef, nor are the hints in this section detailed enough for the reader to determine what the Grail is.

However, the Grail is always carried by a damsel, and it is golden and studded with gems. Parcival is somewhat dismayed and does not realize that he is supposed to ask a question of the Grail. The proper question is, "Whom does one serve with it". In this legend the Grail is allegorically described as being a dish or vessel. But, thusly as a dish or vessel, one may surmise the question is, "Who is intended to eat or drink from it?" Regardless, Parcival fails to ask the 'correct question', and the next morning upon awakening he finds the castle empty. He learns later that because he failed to answer the question, he has caused a 'blight on the land'. Further, he learns that he is part of the Grail family, and the Fisher King was his uncle.

Parcival now declares that he no longer loves God, and can believe in him no more, because of his experience with the Grail.

It has been said that Robert de Boron christianized the Grail in his, 'Roman de l'Estoire dou Saint Graal', written between 1190 and 1199. He claims to draw from an earlier source than Cretienne de Troyes who had written, 'Le Roman de Percival' or 'Le Conte del Graal' in the 1180's. This Grail romance was dedicated to Phillipe d' Alsace, Count of Flanders.

Robert de Boron is the first Grail romancer to give a Grail history. Yet he too, states that the Grail was the cup used at the last supper, which Joseph of Arimathea used to gather the blood of Jeshua ben Jusef after he was removed from the cross. But, since it can be proven historically through the examination of the Gospels that Jeshua ben Jusef did not die on the cross, we must assume that the 'death and resurrection' myth is not only important to preserve, but that the Grail, is *not* a cup, but a cup is allegorical to the Grail. He then goes on to say that Joseph's family became the Guardians of the Grail. He also suggests that Galahad, of Arthurian legend, is the son of Joseph of Arimathea... He states that the Grail was passed to Brons, who is Joseph's brother in law. Brons takes the Grail to England, and the rest is convoluted.

If we compare this to Cretienne's Grail poem, we will see that Percival is the 'son of the widow lady' and he is also the grandson of the Fisher King. So, de Boron makes the statement that Percival is the 'grandson', and in Cretienne's version, Percival is the 'nephew'. Cretienne's story is set in England during the time of Joseph of Arimathea. This strange series of events suggests that, the characters in both stories are not simply characters, but personages who live allegorical lives. And such are the Grail romances, allegorical and initiatory mystery plays to be analysed, experienced and provide a learning experience for the true Seeker.

Wolfram Von Eschenbach is the key writer on the the Grail romances as he does more to isolate and identify the Grail than any of the other romanciers. His 'Parcival' is, as most medieval literature, difficult to read and one must read in between the lines. Von Eschenbach gives all the hints and keys to substantiate 'what' the Grail is. He states that his account is the 'true account', and that it is more than an 'initiatory document'. He states that 'there is more to the Grail mystery than meets the eye'. He states that the Grail is not 'merely an object' of fantasy, but suggests that it is a means of 'hiding a secret of great importance'. He suggests to the reader to 'read between the lines', yet he implies that if the secret is discovered, it 'must be kept a secret'.

He gives several keys to what the Grail is, such as: "For no man can ever win the Grail unless he is known in Heaven and he be called by name to the Grail", and: "The Grail is unknown save to those who have been called by name... to the Grail's company".

Von Eschenbach states that the Grail is that "which supplies what is needed". Getting back to the head of Bran the Blessed, and his cauldron of rebirth and resurrection thought by some to be the Grail and observing the Templars as a cult of the head, we might examine the charges drawn up against them on Aug. 12, 1308. These charges suggest that the Templars had an 'object' or 'objects', namely 'heads' which, 'make riches, make the trees flower, make the land germinate'. These heads were some sort of symbol of death and rebirth, which could 'supply whatever was needed'.

To elaborate more on the cult of the head, there was a curious relic which was confiscated from the Templars in 1307. It was kept in a silver reliquary, shaped like a woman's head and described as beautiful in appearance. Inside was one skull wrapped in linen with a red cloth wrapping over this. There was also a label with 'CAPUT LVIIIm'. The skull is from a small woman. This is the head of Mary of Magdala, and in several accounts it is identified by the name Yse, who is the Princess Goddess of the Grail. Yet, the head used by the Templars was/is a mummified head of a man, often bearded.

It is suggested in 'Parcival' that the Templar Knights lived from a "stone of the purest kind". It was named as 'lapsit exillis', meaning; 'by the power of the stone, the Phoenix burns to ashes, but the ashes give him life again'. Again, the theme of death and rebirth occurs. It also suggests 'immortality'. but, this all suggests the philosophers stone of Alchemical fame. And the Grail is much more than an experiment in Alchemy. But, it could have been cleverly disguised in allegory as the Philosophers Stone.

In 'Parcival' the Grail is suggested as being a 'stone head', and a stone in which the name and lineage is written around the edge of the stone. Here are some very important keys: The keeper of the Grail in Parcival is Reponse de Choix (Chosen Response); Anfortas, the Fisher King and Lord of Grail Castle is wounded in the genitals and unable to procreate for he is under a curse, that though he is the one chosen to guard the Grail, he can never know the love of a woman. Thusly 'he' who is chosen to guard the Grail is 'he' who is unloved by women, and only 'she' who is a pure Grail Princess can break his curse and fall in love with him by the first kiss and her 'chosen response'.

In 'The Temple and the Lodge', by Michael Baigent and Richard Leigh, they correctly refer to Grail Castle as 'Castellum Puellarum' which Geoffrey of Monmouth refers to. Castellum Puellarum translates to ' castle of the childlike woman', which is the perfect description of a Princess.

In Parcival it is stated that maidens are appointed to care for the Grail. It is also suggested that in the Grail family, "The men, God sends forth secretly; the maidens leave openly". In other words, the men keep their lineage secret in the service of the Grail that they may seek out and find Grail women, as the family bloodline has been scattered. The women leave openly that they may identify themselves to Grail men.

Here are some of the hints and keys described by Wolfram Von Eschenbach and other writers which suggest that the Grail is a specific, tangible and absolute element.

1— The Grail is NOT a cup, but is synonymous with a cup.
2— The Grail grants what is needed.
3— One must be pure of heart to carry the Grail.
4—The carriers of the Grail are chosen by God (more specifically T.G.A.O.T.U. and Yse, Princess Goddess).
5— The Grail is associated with death and rebirth.
6— Maidens are appointed to 'care for the Grail'.
7— It may be 'held' in stone heads and engraved in talismanic stones.
8— The Fisher King is he who is unloved by women.
9— The Grail is associated with a Bloodline.
10—The Grail is specifically associated with the bloodline of Jeshua ben Jusef and Joseph of Arimathea.
11—The Grail is associated with a curse, that when broken will restore the 'Wasteland'.
12—The Grail is a repetitive initiatory allegorical mystery.
13—The power of the Grail can make or depose kings, feed the hungry, attract and bring wealth or whatever is needed.
14—One must go through physical and spiritual tests and ordeals in order to prove they are worthy to know the Grail.
15—The secrets of the Grail are always guarded and protected by a secret society, devoted to the protection and guardianship of the Grail.
16—To find the Grail, one must Quest for it and enter into a spiritual initiation in order to begin their Quest.
17—The Grail is proven through Divine Mathematics.

The true Grail has all of these 17 elements included in it. There are many so called 'new-age' interpretations of the Grail and the Quest. They are nothing more than new-age interpretation of Grail literature which is little understood. None of those alleged Grail teachings hold any truth or value beyond teaching a spirituality of the self. Only the Order of the Holy Grail, under jurisdiction of The United Orders of the American Rite has any legal and legitimate lineage and sole rights to the teachings which we have guarded and protected since the beginning.

The Truth about the Crucifixion

Religion fails in many aspects of its aims and promises. Conventional mainstream Christianity teaches about the power of prayer. Yet, imposes conditions of conduct based upon man's, not God's laws, in order to achieve results by prayer. This results in many disappointments as the prayers are never answered. Then the person starts to doubt God because he is not 'listening'. This turns people from God and towards Lucifer.

In reality, God does NOT answer prayers. God does NOT have the power of Divine Intervention. Thus you may rest assured that it is not that God is turning a deaf ear, He simply had never set the design of prayer into the universal cosmos and schema of things. For if this were so, He would simply step in and defeat Lucifer and make all things grand such as existed in the Celestial Realm during the pre-existence.

All of the evil in the world is caused by Lucifer, Lilith and the triple headed Hecate. It is them you should hate for your troubles and those of the world, not God. He appointed his two sons, Michael and Lucifer to fight the battle of good and evil, and gave us all 'free agency of will' to fight for either side. If you are not fighting alongside Michael, you support Lucifer.

Another problem with the church is the idea of the crucifixion. The church says that Jesus 'died' for our sins. How can this be? We are born without sin, and all will return to our Celestial home when the Luciferian Rebellion is over. We were recreated upon this earth (the Terrestrial Realm) for one purpose: to Quest for the Holy Grail, for the purpose of learning the Balance of Perfection. Seeing as God gave us Free Agency of Will, how can we be born in sin. And if, Jesus died for us, and if this removed our sins, why does the conduct of many people range from hurtful to downright evil? No, you were not born in sin, nor are you saved from sin. But sin can be avoided if you side with Michael.

The church also says that 'Jesus will return in the end times. Are people to believe that a man who died almost 2,000 years ago is to return? Yes, this is what they would have you believe. But this is not the case. It is a descendant with pure blood who will return with the message. But, this will only happen when the Marriage of the Bride has been fulfilled and the Curse on the Grail Family is broken and the Wasteland restored.

We Teach:

1- That Jeshua the Teacher (Jeshua ben Jusef) 'lived' for mankind and has created a Divine Bloodline from T.G.A.O.T.U. and Yse, which his descendants carry, that they may be able to more readily fight Lucifer, Lilith and the triple headed Hecate, and win the Grail, so we may all return to the Celestial Realm in True Perfection.
2- That Jeshua the Teacher was born of Joseph and Mary and they were entered by T.G.A.O.T.U. and Yse, Divine Goddess, that Jeshua could be born of Gods and man, that he might have purpose and be set apart from the rest.
3- That the return of Jeshua the Teacher, is not his personage, but one of his bloodline which carries both his blood and that of his natural parents as well as T.G.A.O.T.U. and Yse, Sacred and Divine Goddess.

Jeshua the Teacher (Jesus) escaped the crucifixion to 'live' for us. It is important to realize that Jeshua the Teacher was born of the blood of T.G.A.O.T.U. and Joseph as well as the blood of Yse, Divine Goddess and Mary. He was the first man to be born of the blood of Gods and human. This was the only time God could interfere with mankind. It is to this act that Jeshua had to 'live' for us. So that his descendants could carry the bloodline of the first God and His Goddess wife, that they could fight Lucifer and win back the Holy Grail. These peoples became the Merovingians, who hold the lineage through direct bloodline. They merged with the Arcadians who held the lineage from the priesthood. Both lineages are most important. The next section is a short lecture taken from the Ritual of the Holy Grail.

The Crucifixion

The Grail Priesthood is a continuation of the Melchezedek Priesthood, who were the keepers of the Pactio Secreta (great secret). This priesthood was continued in Rheddae, France and Glastonbury, England by Joseph of Arimathea, who was the founder of the Culdee tradition.

The Grail Priesthood has changed its outer form from time to time to protect itself from its enemy the holy Roman church. It has been hidden within the Culdee, Cathars, Templars, The Crafte and the Illuminati.

The holy Roman church made many attempts to destroy the priesthood with its absurd heresy laws sanctioned by the inquisition. It was not until Adam Weishaupt, professor of canon law at Ingolstadt university had infiltrated the Jesuits, to destroy the inquisition from the inside, so finally we could organize as a priesthood in 1776, under the jurisdiction of the Strict Observance, Knights Templar/Illuminati.

The inquisition lasted from the 5th to the 18th century. They made and enforced laws and the most vile and cruel punishments imaginable to destroy the truth of the Grail, regardless of how it was allegorically hidden. Specifically the heresy laws were aimed at suppression of information which denied the crucifixion. For if the truth came to be known, the church would fall.

This was a constant element of belief within Cathar doctrine which carried into the Templar doctrine. The Knights Templar held the church at bay for several hundred years with threats to expose the crucifixion hoax. And the Templars blackmailed the church for large amounts of money and land with the truth behind their doctrine.

The fact that the crucifixon never took place is a fundamental doctrine within Grail theology, as the opposite myth is fundamental to Christian doctrine. Grail doctrine teaches that Jeshua ben Jusef was Divine, but solely as a Grail Keeper. It teaches that he was able to work his miracles because he could 'activate' and 'direct' the power of the Grail.

Within ordinary life, Jeshua ben Jusef, or Jeshua the Teacher was an ordinary flesh and blood man, who worked, suffered, felt happy and sad as other men do. Yet, his father Joseph of Arimathea and mother Mary, were chosen by T.G.A.O.T.U. and Yse, to inhabit 'spiritually', during his conception. Thus he is the son of man and woman and the son of a God and a Goddess. Thus his blood and bloodline is Divine, and only through it can the Truth be found.

A study of the gospels will turn up some very contradictory facts. The contradictions may have been purposefully inserted in the gospels in order to reveal them under close scrutiny.

Jeshua ben Jusef was arrested by the Sanhedrin, the council of Jewish Elders. This took place during the night of the Passover according to historic record. But, the Sanhedrin were forbidden by Judaic law to meet over the Passover. They were also forbidden to meet at night in private houses or outside the Temple jurisdiction. Yet, records show that they did in fact meet at night to bring Jeshua ben Jusef to Pilate for sentencing.

Jeshua was sentenced to be crucified. But there are specific laws regarding crucifixion in both method and reason, which were not observed!

It is taught that Jeshua ben Jusef died on the cross after a few hours, which is not likely, as a man could last for days on the cross before dying. If the victim lingered too long, the soldiers would break his legs in order to bring on a quick death. This was both common practice and procedure in crucifixion.

Vinegar would be kept on hand to be used to stimulate any victim who was ready to pass out. Yet, Jeshua ben Jusef never has his legs broken, and when he inhales the vinegar he seemingly expires. This suggests that a sponge held a drug that when inhaled would bring on a death like state. It was also common practice to leave the corpse of the victim on the cross to rot. The corpse would be guarded by the soldiers. Yet in the case of Jeshua ben Jusef, his body is removed from the cross and immediately entombed. Not only is this highly unusual and suspicious, but the tomb is privately owned by his father, Joseph of Arimathea.

Contradictions even occur regarding the place of crucifixion. One report is that the crucifixion takes place at Golgotha, the place of the skull which is a barren skull shaped hill. In another account he is said to have been crucified in a garden, wherein the tomb was situated.

These and other biblical hints strongly suggest that Jeshua ben Jusef was not crucified but that the church wanted him to appear so. For by making him their dead martyr, they could collect followers, which meant collecting money. But in any case, it does not make any sense for the bible to contradict the main events surrounding the blood atonement of its major figure.

The Melchezedek Priesthood has always maintained that the crucifixion was a hoax. It had to be faked because of the controversy which surrounded his teachings. It was his way to get out while he could to preserve the truth.

After the crucifixion the disciples were dispersed and ordered to travel and teach the Grail doctrine to new disciples and find the Princesses. Jeshua ben Jusef, Mary of Magdala,

Mary of Bethany, Mary his mother and Joseph of Arimathea his father went to France with the help of Nicodemus. Here Joseph made contact with Celtic Priests who helped the family settle, and in turn he imparted the wisdom of the Grail to them.

The bloodline of Jeshua ben Jusef, which is also the bloodline of Joseph and Mary as well as T.G.A.O.T.U and Yse, being a bloodline of both man and God was preserved and protected by the Priesthood. It is still protected today. This protection has taken many guises over the years in the form of secret societies and priesthoods such as Cathars, Templars and Illuminati. Where you find a Melchezedek Priesthood you will find the crucifixion/hoax doctrine.

Angels and the Spiritual Quest

Angels Among Us!
The Gnostic (Johannine) Christian Path

Angels have been with us since the beginning of mankind. They appear in the theological writings of many religions and in the myth and legend of many cultures. This little booklet will help you to understand Angels from both a Templar Gnostic and a Christian point of view.

In the year 54AD at Rheddae (Rennes le Chateau), France, Joseph of Arimathea received visitations from Angels. They instructed him to write down their account and teach it to the Melchezedek Priesthood. This account was called 'The Book of the Holy Grail' or 'Merovingian Bible'. It was successfully translated into English by Thomas Jefferson in 1787. Each section of the book covers intrinsic elements of God's law as was written in the pre-existence.

According to this work, whose prophet and scribe was the father of Jeshua the Teacher (Jesus), the story of God and the pre-existence was told in the Lesser and Greater Books of the Merovingian Bible. While this doctrine may not correspond with conventional mainstream Christianity in general as is taught in the common translations of the Old and New Testaments, it does indeed shed light on the missing pieces and does in fact agree with the Dead Sea Scrolls, Gnostic Gospels, Pistis Sophia and original Mormon priesthood teachings. But, before you dismiss this account, remember, it is not an account of 'religion', but an account of Angels, which are part of theology.

The Story of the Merovingian Bible goes like this:

At one time there was only God. He was all omnipotent and existed alone. This caused him to become discontented, thus he split himself in two in order to create a mate. He kept the elements of Order and Logic for his own being and gave his mate the elements of Chaos and Emotion for her being. Her name is Yse (pron. Issa). She became so overwhelmed with love at her creation that when he kissed her, she gave him a reaction which was to become known as the 'Chosen Response'. The Chosen Response was the first acknowledgement and reaction of love between a male and female in the universe, and this became the greatest secret of and mystery of mankind, being 'The Holy Grail'.

By comparison to our time frame, this time period is referred to as the pre-existence. God created a world for them to inhabit where they had children who were Gods and Goddesses, being lesser, greater, minor and major within their Divine Dispensations and Holy Ordnances. This place where they lived is referred to as the Celestial Realm.

They were all infinite, immortal and perfect. But, one day grew tired of their perfection. The three oldest sons, being Michael (Jeshua the Teacher), Melchezedek and Adamas (Lucifer) sought council with Heavenly Father on how to correct this discontentment. After some deliberation, Heavenly Father decided that they should have an evolution of development, and should for a time become finite, mortal and imperfect in order for them to appreciate their perfection in the Celestial Realm (Heaven).

Michael agreed with Heavenly Father, but Adamas (Lucifer) rebelled at the idea. Melchezedek remained neutral. Thus ensued the 'war in Heaven', where many sided with Michael and many with Adamas. Those who did not take sides went with Melchezedek. The family was split and Heavenly Father was saddened and angered. He gathered them together and told them that he would make a contest to settle the matter. He would create the Terrestrial Realm (Earth), where they would be reborn as mortal, finite and imperfect beings. That they could, by his permission have free agency of will to follow Michael or Lucifer, likewise Michael and Lucifer could choose people to serve them. He would give Melchezedek authority to create the True Priesthood of God on the Terrestrial Realm. He also made Melchezedek the Prince of the Neutral Angels and all who were under him were made Angels as well.

Within this theology, Melchezedek would take the Holy Grail to Earth. He would create the High Priesthood to guard the Holy Grail. Those who served Michael would guard, protect, preserve and Quest for the Grail. Those of Lucifer would deny the Grail and try to hide it from the world.

Thus, the Terrestrial Realm was created and Heavenly Father became the Great Architect of the Universe, and we were created in the image of Gods (as it states in Genesis). From the beginning, the forces of Lucifer have created many wars, called the Luciferian Rebellion. The Melchezedek Priesthood has undergone three distinct changes. At first they were only High Priests who by faith guarded the Grail, though they knew not what they guarded. It was Jeshua the Teacher (Michael) who instituted the second change to the High Priesthood when he made Mary of Magdala (his favourite disciple) the first High Priestess. The third change came when Joseph of Arimathea created the office of Grail Princess and bestowed it upon Mary of Bethany.

The Princess

The most important person in Grail theology is the Princess. She is a female who is ‘pure of heart’. Essentially she is one who is as the wife of Heavenly Father, who in fact is chosen by Yse. If she gives the Chosen Response to the ‘Fisher King’, when they kiss, and falls in love with him, she will restore the Wasteland and defeat Lucifer. She will also help the Fisher King find the lost and hidden plates which will be translated for the followers of Michael. She has many attributes which are rare in this day and age. She is opposite in body, mind and spirit to the evil Lilith (the hairy night fiend) and the triple headed Hecate, who ‘bellows fire and smoke’, both servants of Lucifer (see Pistis Sophia).

The Grail Princess must be pure of body, mind and spirit. She must not smoke, for according to Gnostic theology, one has ‘sight through their breath’, and this must not be clouded by smoke. Also to smoke, would count her as one who is influenced by the evil triple headed Hecate who bellows ‘smoke and fire’. The element of the Princess is water, and she is watery by nature in body, mind and spirit, and she must take no part in fire, especially a fiery (aggressive) attitude. Prophesy tells us that she knows that she is special, and knows she has a purpose. There is also more than one Princess. As in many Eastern religions, one of the marks of the Princess is decorative body piercing. This is not for fad or fashion, but shows her degree of Holiness and Divinity as a Princess.

Two Forms of Christianity!

Many things are not taught, revealed or are simply mistranslated and misinterpreted in mainstream Christianity. There are gaps and holes and questions left unanswered as the Bible has been translated from the time of the Nicean Trials to the present day.

For instance, many people do not know that there are two distinct forms of Christianity, from the lineage of two disciples, being John and Paul. From Paul we get the 'Pauline Christianity' which most people are familiar with. This form depends upon blind faith, baptism, repentance etc. It is a simple form of Christianity which spans a multitude of Christian denominations, many which strongly disagree with each other.

The lineage from John, being 'Johannine Christianity' is totally different. Rather than simply believing and having blind faith, repentance and baptism, these Christians are 'initiatic' Priests and Priestesses. This means that they go through specific rituals to receive the Divine Ordinances of Heavenly Father. They do not simply read the Bible, they also study the Dead Sea Scrolls, Pistis Sophia, Gnostic Gospels, Merovingian Bible etc. to name just a few of their sacred texts.

Joseph Smith the founder of the Mormon religion was a Gnostic Johannine Christian. In fact true 'original' Mormonism is Gnostic. When he prayed for guidance concerning 'which was the true religion', he was visited by the Angel, Moroni who told him that he *"must join none of them, for they were all wrong, that all their creeds were an abomination in His (God's) sight"*. From his first Angelic visitation, he was genuinely touched by the hand of God.

Joseph Smith was guided to the Hill Cumorah by the Angel Moroni where he dug from the earth 'the Golden Bible', which was later translated into the Book of Mormon. These plates were made of gold and were rectangular and held together by three metal rings. Joseph was also given two stones called the Urim and Thummim by which to translate these plates.

One of the most important elements of the Melchezedek Priesthood is he who is chosen as a Prophet. A Prophet must meet specific criteria, he must be a seer, translator and revelator. All else is secondary to his duties. Prophets are Chosen by God through Angelic communication. A man who is not a seer, translator (i.e. the finding of plates through Angelic instruction) and revelator is not a Prophet.

Joseph Smith and James Jesse Strang were the only Prophets of the Mormon religion. They were the best of friends and Joseph named James his successor as he knew that he would die at Carthage jail in Illinois. The details of the letter of succession appear in the 1848 edition of 'The Diamond'. Both men met the criteria of a Prophet ie. they both found plates and translated them, had Angelic visitations and gave accurate prophesy. Yet many others took over the Church and caused splits and schisms within. People like Brigham Young, Joseph Smith III, Sidney Rigdon, Aldus Cuttler et al, were First Presidents of their respective Mormon groups, but none were prophets in the true sense of the word.

Mormonism was created as a Gnostic Johanine form of Christianity. It was never meant to become a mainstream Pauline form of Christianity. In fact Joseph Smith was adamant about the Saints 'not imitating the Gentile' (ie. Protestant). After all this was the foundation of the Mormon religion.

The most intrinsic elements of true Mormonism have been largely abandoned by all but the most adamant fundamentalist Mormons.

End Times

In this day and age most of the Mormon denominations simply imitate conventional Pauline Christianity and have rejected all of the important elements which made them a unique and tangible religious body with a legitimate Priesthood. The teachings of Joseph Smith are largely ignored in favor of appeasing society with adherence to feminist and politically correct ideology. Many have sold out to the 'laws of man' rather than keeping the 'Laws of God'.

We are currently in the Fullness of Times. The war between good (Michael) and evil (Lucifer) is raging daily. It has destroyed much of our traditional family life, infected society with violence, disease, poverty, apathy as well as a lack of morals and ethics.

While many people *'think'* they are doing *'good'*, they are in fact only behaving in a manner which is subservient to the *'laws of man'*. Many people have opted for a Pauline form of Christianity, without *thinking*. They blindly accept faith, dogma and 'religion', with no idea of spirituality or real theological knowledge or wisdom. They approach Christianity in a closed minded sense of 'self' rather than 'purpose and works'. Yes, it is nice to be good to people and to be kind and generous. But, ask yourself, 'what are you doing to fight Lucifer'? If you are not active in the fight against evil, then he will win. And if that happens, the Angels will no longer come to us. That is the point.

With current economic stresses, people have turned a blind eye towards Lucifer. They feel that they do not have a responsibility to fight against evil. They claim to be good Christians, but are not actively involved in theology. Yes, they go to church, and they pray, but that is not good enough. They feel that blind faith, baptism and *repentance* is good enough. It is not. That is a self serving means to an end. They must become aware of the Fullness of Times. They must 'dare' to be 'called' and perhaps 'chosen'. They must be concerned with the state of mankind, not just themselves, and study prophesy and the revelations of the Bible, and try to understand what is happening. Heavenly Father created this world for us, and created us. We must respect this.

It is important that people open their eyes, hearts, minds and souls to understand the plan of Heavenly Father. We must recognize and know the signs which mark the Fullness of Times. And we must NOT be a part of any ideology which is marked as Lucifer's doctrine by prophesy and revelation.

Evils of the End Times: a hard and fast look at Evil!

Evil, by it's very nature seeks to undermine the work of God. It takes many forms and is not really understood unless it is examined and dissected. If you have not been taught to do this, chances are that you support some evil ideologies. of course you don't want to hear this, but read on and *'think'*, you were given 'free agency of will' by God. Now is not the time to be high and mighty, thinking that evil can't affect you.

Even going around saying certain things are evil, because you don't like them, or supporting a politically correct agenda is a form of evil. For instance, many good Christians tout the idea that Halloween is evil! They claim it has to do with the Devil and Satan. Quite frankly this is a theological and historical fallacy.

Halloween is All Hallows Eve, the night before All Saints Day. This was, in the Celtic culture, their new year. At this time of the year it was legend that the spirits of the dead could return to earth and watch over their relatives, friends etc. People would dress as their deceased relatives in order to walk among the spirits undetected.

It was Hollywood and the greed of commercialism which turned Halloween into a scary and evil night. And Hollywood, greed and commercialism as far as I know has *no* jurisdiction over anything Divine, so why pay homage to these tainted ideas by believing them as gospel!

On the other side of the coin, all Christians celebrate Easter, without the knowledge that the same Celtic peoples were the originators of the holiday. Easter was first the holiday of Eostre, which was a celebration of death, rebirth and fertility, of the old Pagan God, called the Green Man. Pauline Christians do not know this, but the church successfully placed the idea of the 'resurrection' over this holiday so the converts could become comfortable with the resurrection.

Likewise, Pauline Christians are not aware that they all stem from the holy Roman church, which when it invaded the Celtic lands, particularly Britain, would infiltrate its ideas onto the Celtic religious culture in order to convert them. They created all of the popular Christian holidays over Celtic holidays. We are not suggesting that the ancient Celts were evil, they were simply different. The two examples shown above, are both researchable both theologically and historically. They illustrate how uninformed many churches keep their members, and can in fact scare and control members in the case of the Halloween myth.

So, is a thing evil because a minister says it is? If you are told a thing is evil, when it is not, are you not being deceived and *'bearing false witness"*?

Evil comes in many disguises. It can be power, deceit and control by a church, government, political agenda etc. It can be attractive to some people such as greed, drugs, indulgence etc. It also can be blatant such as in crime, violence, murder etc.

In any respect, evil is always marked by the 'easy path' which is the first temptation. For instance it is easy to become bitter and carry hatred after an emotional devastation. It is difficult to turn to God and pray for help. This is because the 'evil' of the situation wants to 'keep you down' and bound to its powers. You must learn to recognize evil for what it is and fight it on a daily basis. Evil also has a second temptation, 'power'.

Feminism is one of the greatest evils of our time. Its foul ideology has destroyed churches, marriages, families and relationships. Feminism is based on 'power and control'. Gullible women who are bitter and filled with hatred swarm like flies to this ideology for the power it gives them to control and destroy. Society by man's law, advocates this and supports it with its man made laws. Where there is power, there is always the chance of corruption. As it has been said, 'power corrupts and absolute power corrupts absolutely'. It is interesting that feminism is directly linked to smoking in its ideology even from the time of the suffragettes to present day advertising. Even more interesting is the link to the triple headed Hecate who 'bellows smoke and fire', and how Hecate is the patron of many neo-pagan goddess cults, all which tout feminism as part of their political agenda. That, is a true examination of evil.

Personal power is an evil of Lucifer. It is 'attractive', especially to embittered women, and those who are too young to understand that 'power must be tempered by respect and it must be quenched by discipline'. As we have discussed, the triple headed Hecate and Lilith the hairy night fiend are evil deities. These are two primary demonesses who are worshipped by many neo-pagan feminist goddess cults, which in most of its denominations subjugates men. Hecate and Lilith are portrayed as 'mother goddesses'. The truth is not told, as like in many Christian denominations. They who worship Lilith and Hecate, who are both demonesses who have very evil attributions, are devil worshippers. But the leaders don't tell this to their followers.

A Chosen Language, Chosen Peoples and a Chosen Land

The Merovingian Bible, which is the sacred writings of Joseph of Aramathea, imparted to him by the Neutral Angels states that Divine Mathematics correspond to the Chosen Language. The Chosen Language will be spoken in the Chosen Land, by the Chosen peoples. All of this prophesy points to the English language and America when examined closely. The Divine Mathematics of God will also be used to be able to prove the elements of the Holy Grail and the ways of the Divine Princess. This only applies to English. Prophesy also states that the followers of Lucifer and the triple headed Hecate will try to destroy the Chosen Language so that its words which describe the Princess will be hated by the women who are possessed by the evil of these two demons. of course, those words are gentle and feminine words which are opposite to feminist words to describe a female.

This brings us to a great evil which is as bad as feminism and that is the politically correct ideology. Also, like feminism, this evil has the ability to convince the spiritually weak, that it is a 'good thing'. Even George Orwell, a prophet in his own right, in his book *Nineteen Eighty-Four*, told about social control and Newspeak, which was/is the same as the politically correct Newspeak.

Politically correct ideology was touted by new-age guru, Dick Sutfen who said that politically correct ideology could be easily 'infiltrated' into society. Then the New-Agers could take over. Politically correct words, meanings, terms etc. are all prejudicial towards traditional religious practices and traditional lifestyles. The wording is geared to 'disguise' truth. It is essentially a new language of confusion and deception. It takes reality and makes it into 'new-age whimsy'. This causes people to let down their defenses and become weak in mind and spirit. In turn, it allows the Luciferian ideology of New-Ageism to be slowly absorbed into society. It is the Tower of Babel story repeated.

Many Christian churches have been subject to new-ageism, and not even been aware of it. The Church of Jesus Christ of Latter Day Saints–Utah has fallen victim to this when the Endowment House Rites were changed due to feminists objecting to the content and wording in 1990. The United Church years before was bombarded by feminist ideology causing break ups in the church. So, even the church, as a whole, is not exempt from evil influence. Evil creeps in when you let your guard down, and don't keep an eye out for it, especially when you subscribe to man's law and popular opinion rather than God's law and spiritual facts.

Princesses—The Most Important Aspect of the Holy Grail

The key to understanding the riddle of the Holy Grail, and the main key to the Quest is the Princesses. Without them there would be no Holy Grail. The riddles to discovering the Princesses are hidden in the Merovingian Bible in the 2nd Book of Joseph the Patriarch, Book of Amberis and Book of Varena.

Within these three books, her riddle is hidden for you to discover. The Princess, in her own right is an enigma. A Grail Princess can not be 'made', she simply 'is', that is to say, you can not take any female, give her a set of instructions and turn her into a Princess. For if this were the case, we would have many Princesses and the Wasteland would have been restored eons ago.

She who is a Princess is born with certain attributes. She is chosen by Yse, Divine and Sacred Goddess, and her virtues and qualities are instinctual and natural. She who is chosen by Yse to be a Princess may not even know she is one. This fits into the aspect of the Grail where the Grail Maidens (Princesses) may hold and guard the Grail, yet not know they perform this function.

The Royal Grail Princess is above a Grail Priestess, who must also have Princess qualities, yet she may not be the one to break the Curse on the Grail Family. Princesses are more akin to being representatives of the Goddess Yse, on earth. There are a certain set of standards of behavior which are intrinsic to a Princess, which are patterned after the virtues of Yse. First and foremost of these is that she must be opposite to Lilith the hairy night fiend and the triple headed Hecate. This mystery must be uncovered by her and displayed by her by action. She who is a Princess goes through a most important transformation from mortal to Divine. Here she will discover the riddle of 'water', for she is only water and never fire. She must not have fire in her temper nor may she smoke, for even these two things will destroy any of her watery energy current. The name Mary, literally means 'water'.

Her general disposition is very gentle, calm, passive. She needs no aggression, no fire. She is at peace with her goddess qualities. Part of her riddle is that she inhabits Castellum Puellarum, which is Grail Castle. All of her virtues and qualities are proven by Divine Mathematics and the Grail Equation is present in her words which are of the Chosen Language. Prophesy teaches us that in the Fullness of Times the evil of Lilith and the triple headed Hecate will try and destroy and demean the words which are sacred to the Princess. This has come about through feminist ideology which deplores Princess qualities, and through politically correct new-speak many of her words have been assigned undesirable qualities. This is all part of the Luciferian Rebellion's plan to destroy any trace of the Princess in females so it can not manifest in society. Thus, many females serve evil without knowing that they do so. While you may pick the side i.e.. good or evil, which you want to fight for, know that good or evil can also choose you, and you can serve without knowing your master.

Joseph of Arimathea instituted the position of Princess in order to have a manner in which the Curse on the Grail family may be lifted. He did this by writing our most sacred ritual known as The Sacred Marriage of the Elements, which is al allegory of the first act of love when T.G.A.O.T.U. kissed Yse, Sacred Goddess and she gave the Chosen Response.

It is foretold that in the Fullness of Times that a Princess would come which would lead us to metal plates buried in the earth which would be translated by the Patriarch. That these plates would establish much of our Templar doctrine. They were buried in America by Templars and the cycle will be complete for the Marriage of the Bride, when they are unearthed by her, that then, the time for the real work will be at hand.

The details are covered in the Book of Joseph the Patriarch, Book Five. The following is a short version of the story of the Curse as taken from the Merovingian Bible, according to Brons.

The Story of the Curse

I, Brons, will reveal the tragic and sad account of the Curse placed upon Joseph the Younger, by Jeshua the Teacher, also called Joseph the Teacher in this new land. It had been decreed by God that the First Divine Family escape the First Chosen Land and be removed unto the Second Chosen Land, there to establish the High Priesthood within the family and keep it by bloodline. And this task was fraught with obstacles and ordeals for the Divine Family, whose task it was to find husbands and wives for their grown children.

Those who were not yet prepared for the Royal Marriage, were bound to the study of the High Priesthood and turn away their lower passions. Yet they were encouraged to look for any who would make a suitable husband or wife, and enter the High Priesthood. And here, the Patriarch would test they who were chosen to wed, and be they found worthy, the wedding feast would be arranged.

And all were warned not to give in to the lower passions, but to seek only those men and women chosen by the Holy Grail, to keep company with and wed. Here and only here was it not against God and Yse for them to know the passions of their loins.

Yet, the son of Joseph the Teacher, being Joseph the Younger, in his 17th. year, was a High Priest of such a degree which had not ever been known before. And Joseph the First, had chosen him to be Keeper of the Holy Grail, after Joseph the Teacher.

Yet Joseph the Younger was a strong and vigorous man whose talents were many, and whose days were not long enough to fit therein all the tasks he would wish to undertake. And he was given to the lower passions and had been warned many a time never to stray from his duty to the High Priesthood and the Holy Grail.

After long hours of work with his father, he would rest a few hours with his companions, and they would drink and feast and discuss their trades, lives and the Priesthood.

And there came to the tavern where they often met, a girl of delightful beauty. And Joseph the Younger turned his attentions to her. And she was, by nature and instinct, of Yse, but had not been consecrated. And this she should have been, and he should have taken her to the Patriarch and the High Priesthood, and as I know, would have been consecrated as a Princess. But, Joseph did not act in wisdom but in folly. And he caused her to become big with child.

And when word of this reached Joseph the Teacher, he became angry, to the likes of which none had ever witnessed, and he vowed to curse his son for eternity. For not only had Joseph the Younger gone astray from his duty, but he had also ruined a girl who would have become a Princess if she had ever been consecrated.

For, now she was soiled by child, who, because she was not made a Princess, could not carry the bloodline.

And Joseph the Teacher cursed his son to walk his many lives without the love of a woman, to be bound to strict duty to the High Priesthood forever. And to the girl, he placed this curse, that none would desire her or love her, until she was possessed by the Spirit of Yse, and in another life found he who was once Joseph the Younger, and fell in love with him and return to him the Chosen Response. Whereby he would consecrate her and make her the Princess she was intended by God to be.

And knowing this curse to be harsh, but having no authority to put an end to it, Joseph the First created the First Ritual of the Grail Priesthood, which was the Marriage of the Elements. Herein, he would provide for Joseph the Younger, a manner in which the curse could be broken, as this Ritual contains all of the Mysteries of the Holy Grail. It is our Foundation

Ritual, and therein be found the design to fulfil the Bargain of the Curse.

That being, Joseph the Younger never being allowed the love of a woman, that by this he is wounded in the genitals and never allowed to die. But he must incarnate and live for many lifetimes and search for Her who will cleave unto him with her love, and give him the Chosen Response. And Joseph the First, knowing this, created the Ritual of the Marriage of the Elements knowing that Joseph the Younger, in his many incarnations would serve the Grail Priesthood. And in so doing, would have the obligation to perform this ritual. And it being the only manner in which he would have the chance to kiss a woman. And herein, if she were to give him the Chosen Response upon being kissed, it would be as Yse, giving Her Response to Her Divine Husband, as a sign of Her love for Him.

And if such were to occur, the Bargain of the Curse would be fulfilled, and Joseph the Younger would be allowed to die. And then the Holy Grail could manifest at the feet of all females who are Pure of Heart, and the Wastelands will be restored. And at this time, the Luciferian Rebellion will be defeated and cease to have power.

(end of account)

Ordo Templis Leonise or Order of the Lion

Liber De Mythologium

The Order of the Lion: Also known as; The Order of the Lion of St. Michael; The Order of the Lion of Judah; The Order of the Lion of the Temple of New Jerusalem; and Order of the Lion of Melchezedek. Is a Knightly Order which separated from the Chivalric Order of the Lion, after WWII.

The section of the society which had been since the beginning of the 2nd millennium, a center of esoteric studies and mystery school originating in Elbashan in Albania as the concealed concord and overlapped with the Hellenism of the Florentine and Mistraian circles, since the 12th century it has been a safe haven for 'the Templar Families' being the 13th tribe of Arcadia, descendents of the Hasidim who were the followers and family of James the Righteous known both as Jewish Christians, the Desposini, descendants of Jesus a thousand suns from the great central sun Melchezidek!

The Heraldic design of the Lion has been an ensign of the ruling families of Europe, Asia and America for several hundred years. The twin pools of Masonic Templarism and Illuminism have their origin within the ranks of the Templar families of the Order of the Lion as a vehicle for gathering up the lost seeds of the bloodlines of Templar clans which have been dispersed as sparks, flames of gold dust upon a sandy beach. But when collected, shine as the suns flame, Melchezedek the Serap of the Messiah reflecting the glory of the Noetos Helios, the intelligible Sun of the father of life. For the Templar families once again joined together are the 2nd coming of Christ.

Our society is governed by what we call Temple Masters,

each with a first and second son assisted by five Priors and five Knights Levites who possess the Fullness of the Covenant. In Europe their exists one Temple Master each of the European cultural language groups of western Christendom.

In North America there are 13 Monasteries near the following cities and areas each governed by a T.M. (Temple Master):

1— The Sphere— North Carolina USA
2— The Gryphon— Niagara Falls, New York, USA
3— The Star— Morgantown, West Virginia, USA
4— The Lion— outside San Diego, California, USA
5— The Triangle— San Antonio, Texas USA
6— The Campus— outside Chicago, Illinois USA
7— The Stag— Arkansas USA
8— The Eye and Pyramid— Tacoma, Washington USA
9— The Rose & Sword— Ross, Nova Scotia, Canada
10— The Double Headed Eagle— Seattle, Washington USA
11— The Document— Virginia USA
12— The Druid— New England, USA
13— The Bell— Philadelphia, Pennsylvania USA

History

The Order of the Lion emerged from a development of the Order of the Phoenix. It is widely known that the three monastic knightly orders wore the three colors of the alchemical process.

The origin of the Order of the Lion is shrouded in the misty veils of antiquity. The myths of the Order have said it originated in the pre-chivalric traditions of the Roman legions of the west as a variant of the mythos of the Danubian Riders and the Tracio-Sarmation mysteries. It was taken to Gaul, thence to Britain and the Irish monasteries. In fact, Arthur comes from Arturus, he of the bear, as the Arcadians are with the people of the bear standard. Arthur was Grand Master, or Father of Fathers, of the Christianized Celto-Roman military sect (connected with the Holy Grail) from whence the Order of the Lion is descended.

It was first brought into Gaul with the restoration of Dagobert II from the Irish monasteries and England through the empire of Charlemagne to the Order of the Lion to equal the mystery school of the eastern empire of Constantinople. By recreating the mysteries of Mithras in the Christianized form from Michael, the Lion of Judah and the great goddess as Mary, the Mother of the church (the Black Rose of Sharron), he sought to renovate the Roman Empire in a Europe-wide model. But his plans were evaporated when Henry II succeeded him. After which the Order of the Lion of St. Michael carried on his agenda in secret.

Since the reign of John the Second of Jerusalem and Cyprius who within his life also became Empirie of Constantinople, the title of the Prince Regent of Romania and Hierusalem, and protector of the Holy Sepulcher, Hierophant and Basilarius-Archton, has been held by the Grand Master of the Order. The leadership of the Order of the Lion, holder of the lineage or bloodline of the Empire of the Hidden Church which descended from; John II to Jaques de Molay who was succeeded by Robert the Bruce as Grand Master of the Order of the Lion.

At the same time de Molay gave leadership to three successions of the Merovingian bloodline, John Mark Larmenius, Peter d' Aumont and his nephew Count Beaujeau who were also all members of the Order of the Lion.

The leadership of the Order of the Lion was connected to the leadership of the Priory of Sion for several centuries until Maximillian Von Hapsburg-Loraine, from whence it passed into the obscure Croatian family of Jelasic for about a century. To Joseph Jelasic Von Buzin in the mid 1800's. In the 1980's, Jelasic O.L.C & M.T.G, through the intercession of his cousin

Thomaslav passed the leadership of the Order of the Lion into the hands of the American Grand Master of the Strict Observance Templar Illuminati and Priory of Sion, and the Patriarch of the Merovingian Templar Gnostic Church O.L. & M.T.G.

Thomaslav who had taken the name Father Jacob O.L. & M.T.G. and Father Adam O.L. & M.T.G. are both holders of the Covenant grade of the Order of the Knight Levite formed with the Council of 3 for the governing of the Order.

The Order of the Lion's esoteric system is not Cabbalistic, but European and is based upon the great school of the Steppe from whence the Hurrian Hykos-Nuzi tribes of Israel and Judah were descended. The basis of our theurgic system is the 26 letters of the European alphabet and the Ramsey's Computus or Diagram, twice thirteen Saphires for each of the three-fold worlds. The Three Fountains of European-esotericism originating from the Order of the Lion were the Strict Observance and the Illuminati which have their origins in the ranks of Templar families.

As well as the pre-Crowlean Ordo Templi Orientis, called the 2nd and 3rd foundation of the of the first foundation being that of the Nine Poor Knights. With regards to the 3rd foundation or the O.T.O. the O.H.O. was originally supposed to develop 5 ethnic bodies; an English, a Teutonic, a French and Slavic, the Romance were developed before his regrettable conversion to the revelation of Thelema. When Reuss adopted the pseudo G.D., Crowlean religion, the Templar Merovingian families whose esoteric lineages were Syrian, Iranian and European in origin dropped the project of the 3rd foundation (the O.T.O. project) as they had the 2nd foundation when the problems occurred with the 3rd.

During the period between the world wars, the esoteric center of the Templar families moved to North America from Europe and 13 esoteric monasteries were established governed by 13 Temple masters chosen to lead the Merovingian race and disseminate its Templar wisdom.

The society is divided into 3 houses of 5 grades each. The House of the Initiate, House of the Adept and House of the Knight Levite. The three Houses wear the alchemistical colors of white, black and red consisting of the innermost House of the Covenant of Arcadia, the outer House of the Lion and the middle House of the Phoenix consisting of Azoth Igniss and the mystical flame of the Internal Sun Bolcho-Set (the Kolob of the Monarchs) and I.H.V.H. of the Jews.

Grades of the Houses

House of Arcadia

Illuminatus Dominus (Rex), Consularus (Regent), Peritus (Majester), Exercitatus (Practricius), Contemplatus (Theoreticus)

House of the Phoenix

Consecrated and Professed Knight of the Temple, Presbeter Knight of the Pelican, Deacon Knight of Hierusalem, Scotch Knight of the Eagle of St. John, Master Knight of the East and St. Andrew.

House of the Initiate

Interior Initiate, Novice Initiate, Novice and two Probationary Grades.

The achievement of the first house is the development of man's latent powers and the introduction to the practices of the knighthood and craftsmanship and the basic tenets of the sect.

The achievement of the 2nd house is the acquiring of the faculty of Abrac (the ability to manifest the Grail in one's life which is one of the powers of the Priesthood of Melchezedek).

The third house is that of the covenant which may not be discussed with the profane save it is in the secret areopagent of the College Royal Sanctitum of the 32 paths to Deity. And only amongst those who have discovered the secret of the Holy Grail.

It was decided upon by the three governors of the Order that the world is now ready for the secret teachings of the O.T.L Due to this being the end of days, it is necessary to re-establish the Order of the Black Rose of Sharron, holders of the true mysteries of the true mysteries of womankind, who fight against the evil mysteries of the vampiric Lilith the hairy night fiend, the triple headed Hecate who bellows smoke and fire and Lucifer.

The House of Arcadia
(The Mercier Doctrine)

Preface

The following account is the testimonial of an ancient family. A family which is both cursed and has a deep rooted spiritual need to preserve their bloodline for the good of mankind. The document that this account is taken from is definitely authentic according to it's purported age as well as the information it contains, which by lineage is also irrefutably authentic.

This is the account, in part of not only an ancient family, but an ancient race of people, who unlike the so-called norm of the population, require a specific bloodline to sustain life. This is perhaps the only published account of this family and race, which is that of the Arcadians, in their language, Yaeras and their secret brotherhood called The Order of the Lion.

But they are not like the rest of us. They are a vital, charismatic, multi talented, sensual race of 'people' whose family lineage is firmly rooted, defined, yet dying. They are the people who are directly related to the Gods of the Pre-Existence, born with the blood of Gods and man, as opposed to simply man. That is the purpose of this book. To collect the families together, to bring those into the family who were there in past incarnations.

The account written in this book in 1858, is the account of the Elders of the bloodline. It is an attempt to solidify the family and its purpose. To present the race customs and family traditions to those who are of Arcadia, but who have fallen from their purpose into common society. The account is a record which bears testimony to the dying out of this beautiful race, and an attempt to preserve it. But also an attempt to solidify and define it for future generations.

The story may disturb some people with it's 'Biblical' story references, and lack of typical occult/esoteric drama and intrigue. It is hoped that people can transcend this prejudice in favor of truth and explanation. In fact one will have to understand some history of both the Cathars and Templars to fully comprehend what they are in fact reading. For, within the story are many keys and riddles, written between the lines. Yet the true Arcadian will understand.

The true Arcadian need not be a direct blood relative. He or she need only be a 'blood' relative through reincarnation, and understand what they read as a part of them, which has been lost and, now refound.

The Arcadian Bloodline Story

The story begins with the first criminal act of murder, when Caine slew Abel. Caine and Abel were the sons of Adam and Eve. Both Caine and Abel made offerings to Rex Mundi, King of the World or 'God'.

God accepted Abel's offering, but refused Caine's. Caine became angry and murdered his brother Abel, thus the first blood was spilled upon the earth, and thus Rex Mundi (God) cursed the earth and made it into a wasteland.

Caine, being terrified that he would be murdered himself for his actions, sought out God and told him this. Caine was cast out of the world (made an outcast), yet marked so he would be known and would not be killed for his actions. With this mark those who would attempt to kill him would be warned that they would feel his wrath seven fold.

Caine was in fact not Adams son, but the son of the spirit Samael. When Adam rejected the evil and repulsive Lilith for marriage in favor for Eve, she contrived to give him her son, and thus destroy his bloodline.

Caine was the son of Lilith (the hairy night fiend) and Samael, the serpent of the garden. Samael gave Caine to Eve, her thinking that the 'Lord' had given her a son.

After the murder, when Caine was cast out to walk the earth forever, he went to the land of Nod, married and had a son named Enoch. Enoch rebelled against his father and mother for his father's crime. He wished to preserve the lineage of Adam, and sought out the Priesthood of Melchezidek, and reestablished himself in Adam's bloodline through the lineage of the Priesthood.

To preserve the lineage, Enoch was given a 'blood rite', which would insure that the family of Adam would always be strong and survive the wrath of Lilith. With this blood rite, ancient knowledge and wisdom could be preserved through reincarnation. Thus where the idea of bloodline immortality comes from.

The bloodline would be different from others, having the ability to remember elements of the past such as talent and ability, intelligence, strength etc. Yet they would be for the most part, a dark and depressed peoples more at home in the dark warmth of the night than to be exposed to their enemies in the light of day

They could 'adopt' or 'create' others like them through the blood rite, and the more they created, the stronger they would become. And the 'creators' would do the blood rite together, and become bound as 'family', and the strength of the bloodline would become strong and they could survive the wrath of Lilith on the world.

The First Elder of the family, in 1858 met with the Council of Elders, to preserve the bloodline because he was convinced that it would soon die and Lilith would ravage the world in her revenge against Adam. What was so frightening to them was the prophesy that if the bloodline was not restored to a direct family lineage before the turn of the year 2000 with many female children born into the bloodline, Lilith could not be slain.

If this did not come to pass, Lilith would curse the blood of mankind with a plague so devastating, none would even dare share blood. And the race of Vampyre would die, and the death of Abel would not be avenged, and with this, the earth would also die.

One can see by this encapsulated short version of the Arcadian myth/legend/religion of the bloodline a complete worldview and complexity regarding the underlying nature of the Arcadian tradition. One can now regard the race as good people, yet outcasts from society, which in fact, serve to fight evil (Lilith and Lucifer)).

Perhaps the Arcadians will win over Lilith. It is already 1977, with only 23 years to defeat the hairy night fiend. Perhaps, hopefully she has already been defeated. We have no great plague upon us, in which Lilith could be undeniably associated with. Maybe, just maybe, the bloodline has survived, but the earth is being destroyed daily, so perhaps she has not been defeated and we will feel the wrath of her blood plague. We will know in 23 years.

Ed. Note This is the introduction to the 1977 edition of this book which was only circulated within the families and close friends of the Arcadian peoples. The current edition, is intended for general distribution to the public as the end is at hand.

Introduction to the 1858 Manuscript

Sons and daughters of Arcadia it is with a great sadness upon my heart that I write these words. The burden of our race and its families has been heavy. Many have refused their birthright and heritage and have left our fold. Others have been brave and have died valiantly to protect our bloodline and noble family. We have been persecuted by the holy roman church for as long as they have existed. We have hidden from their hideous inquisition. We have been outcasts. Thusly I have prepared this manuscript that each family would have one as its lineage demands, lest we ever forget who and what we are. Be proud of your lineage, but hide it from all who are not of the blood. For those of the common publick understand not our purpose and that we are not enemies of them, but are friends as only we can put a stop to that which will be visited unto the world.

Yet we have endured as a peoples, and have kept our ways alive and well. For two hundred years we have lived in this land and have here established ourself as publick citizens. But now the time has come to face the prophecies which have been handed down by our forefathers and Elders. Remember, dear sons and daughters, our ancient ways and teachings. Do not falter in your purpose.

Our house is an ancient one indeed. And through the centuries it has fallen into ruination, yet its foundation is strong and characteristick of our strength to survive. We are different than others, and many detect this difference. Our house is ancient and of the San Graal, and the blood which now runs in your veins had also run in the veins of Adam, Seth, Enoch, Melchezidek, and Joseph in the Holy Land. And then in Europe the blood of Joseph again and his son Jeshua in a continuous bloodline unto the Visigoth Princess Giselle de Razes who married Dagobert II whose bloodline carries on to Hugh de Chaumont and Adelaide de Mercier who was the aunt (and a Grail Princess) of Hugh de Payens, the Grand Master of the Order of the Knights Templar.

It is by our Grail Rite that we have endured and preserved our power as the protectors of the sacred family. That each of us has the blood of our ancestors within us, that we may carry their wisdom and have them with us always. That by this we are not one, but many, for this is our way.

And now a time of sadness and despair falls upon us. I have gazed with the stones and seen a great plague fall upon the earth. This plague is wrought by Lilith to destroy the sacred family which we protect. This plague will destroy blood, thus our bloodline is in danger, as we will be greatly afraid of this plague which will run in the veins of many. And they of this plague and affliction will celebrate their disease, and carry it to many of mankind not of their evil ways. And Lilith will guide them, and none will resist, and many innocent people will die an agonizing death of pain, sores and pustules. And both those afflicted and those whose blood is pure will tolerate and celebrate this madness. And where there is blood, there will be fear as the minions of Lilith spread their disease to all parts of the world in pride and disconcern. And a man of lineage shall be born who is an ancient soul and Patriarch, and should he ever have daughters of the bloodline it will be a sign that a cure shall be found for the plague, and all will right itself. But Lilith will do all in her power from ever allowing any woman to love and cherish this man, for she fears his daughters. And Lilith will destroy the ways of women, and turn them as men to destroy their feminine disposition. And the demoness will slowly dominate and possess their minds and souls and bodies with fire.

We are descended from several families of the tribe of Benjamin, and therein be much of our history and lineage. And that our tribe was cursed and we were cast out from ten of the tribes of Israel for trying to steal from them a woman who could have destroyed the curse of Lilith. We became hunted down and killed by them and became at war with them, and they killed our women so we would die out. But the tribe of Ephraim who did not take part in this war, befriended us as they were at first a neutral tribe. Our tribe was almost completely destroyed, with only a small number of men remaining. The tribe of Ephraim knew full well of the task we were burdened with, and its importance in the world. They allowed those of us who survived to take several wives that our bloodline could be preserved.

Even through this act of kindness and brotherhood, did we give birth to the great King Saul who ruled over Israel and in war against the Ammonites and Amalecites did vanquish. Yet we fell at Gelboeh at the hands of the damnable Philistines.

And many of us escaped and fled to Greece, to Arcadia where we settled and collected our bloodline that we could be strong against Lilith and Lucifer. And thereafter being driven out, we had come into contact with the Gnostics and hid amongst them, and we were protected by the Desposini whose first Bishop was Saint Jaques, whose brother Joseph II (Jeshua the Teacher or Jesus) cursed his son, as Rex Mundi cursed Caine. That the son of Joseph II would walk the earth forever without ever knowing the love of a woman, and that if one ever loved him, the wasteland which Rex Mundi cursed the world as his revenge against Caine for his murder of Abel would be restored to a fruitful and good place without murder, violence, strife, war, disease and starvation. And this unknown Patriarch is above us all and the head of both tribes that of Merovee and that of Arcadia.

Of the most important families of our lineage are the parents of Mary, wife of Joseph I, who were Joachim and Anna, another came from Elizabeth and again another from Cleophas who were cousins of Mary. Yet only those descended from Mary were of the blood of the Desposini. The lineage of Joseph I and Joseph II is a hidden lineage, related to the house of Arcadia and Merovee by direct bloodline and not through the Grail Rite, and it is their Patriarch we protect. But we are no longer of the tribe of Benjamin and Ephraim, we are the 13th tribe which is that of Arcadia. And it is to the houses of Arcadia and Merovee which we swear fealty, to seek the Princesses and protect the bloodline and Elders. And we do this by way of our blood, that we may keep the strength and wisdom of our ancestors within our veins.

You must never forget your purpose and the reason you live. Never even forget your lineage or heritage or customs. For now, as we approach the time of reckoning, though we are few in numbers and tired and weak from centuries of warfare, we must now be stronger than ever before. We must find the hidden Patriarch and break his curse, that we may all survive the plague of blood and the wrath of Lilith. Time is short, our families are scattered and we need to come together that we may continue in strength. It is to that end that I have set down our customs and purpose as a manuscript of study, that more Arcadians may be created. And here I have set down the rules by which we may accomplish this task. By these rules you shall know each other, for now is the time to rebuild and organize.

—Henri Chaumont-Mercier 1858 Boston Mass.

Prophecy of Evil and Sadness

of Evil

¶Beware the signs and omens of evil. Know that you live by the bonding of blood, and that when the wrath of Lilith comes to the earth, you shall die, for much blood will be poisoned and contain her soul and destroy you. And her plague is a mighty plague, which will sweep the land with a vengance, not seen since the plague of Europe. But as we defeated her then, be it known that we can defeat her again.

¶Know that there will be agents of Lilith who carry her plague and will spread it knowing that they bring a horrible death to those they touch. Know also that many innocents will carry her plague, but not her soul, yet they will suffer at the touch of her hairy hand.

¶Know that those who celebrate the blood plague of Lilith are themselves acursed and an evil upon the land, and must be shunned, for they represent a house of great evil.

¶And in fact they are demons of Lilith who go against the natural way of any bloodline. Yet many of them will seem as common people, yet others will be detected by their actions and their dress and the banner which they fly.

¶Know that there will be created a great war between the agents of Lilith and Lucifer wrought against both common people and Arcadians. And many first generation Arcadians will turn renegade and accept the carriers of the blood plague, they will be cast out from their houses and belong to no house as they are weak minded. Only the strongest of our houses will be able to turn their backs on the carriers of the plague.

¶But know that many carriers of the blood plague do not wish to be evil, though they revel in the ways and the customs of Lilith. Know that they are but weak minded and can not fight her. And those who gain strength of mind, will be cured miraculously as a blind man would regain his sight if touched by the hand of God.

¶Know that the blood plague is a sign of the end of mankind and the beginning of an age of falsehood and deception, strife, war, famine, disease and tyranny. And it is to this end that we fight to preserve our world.

¶For with these signs and omens, even the earth itself will grow weak and diseased, and in a state of meloncholia will give up its fight for life.

¶For in this time, up will become down, down will become up, good will become evil, evil will become good. And all will be confusion. And the bloodlines will be outcasts even more than ever before in history, for we will fight for the good, but be perceived as evil for the common people will not understand the true evil, and the purpose of life.

¶Know also that Lilith will visit a curse upon both men and women of weak will, and will reverse them that you will not be able to tell a man from a woman by their nature. And a great strife will be visited upon husbands and wives in the manner of confusion of their true natures. And to this end their children shall be raised in confusion.

¶And there shall be generations born to accept these flaws and evils as the natural order of men and women, though they oppose the races of male and female. And then up will be down, down will be up and good will become evil and evil will become good.

¶And here, will be the biggest challenge of all, even greater than in all history before, and it would be as trying to convince a cat not to chase a mouse. And only those of Arcadia, who were of Arcadia in past lives of incarnation will detect this and shun the ways of the common publick for the truth.

¶And many of these things will come to pass in order to destroy the true nature of woman, that we may not restore the wasteland by the Royal Marriage of the Sacred Princesses to the Patriarch that he may have daughters in that era of time.

¶Teach these prophesies to your children, and they to their children for generation after generation, that when the Patriarch is found, there will be wives for him to choose, that they who are pure of the blood will know and choose him. And then the daughters will be born who will fight and destroy the curse of Lilith.

¶Know that it will be a great task to find and discover the Patriarch as he may not know of us. Know that he is of our blood and the blood of the ancient Houses of Arcadia, and chosen by God, who we protect and are above us. Know that he can lead us and through love deliver us from the curse of Lilith the hairy and ugly one who despises the beauty of women.

of Sadness

¶Know that during this time of Lilith's wrath, many of us will come together again, and they shall be those who have incarnated many times as Arcadians.

¶Know that the powers of Lilith and Lucifer are great and will visit war and destruction unto many thousands of people, only to carry out the destruction of one person.

¶We are about to see civil war in this land. It will come to pass and will be the beginning of the end. Not only will our own families be torn asunder and our own peoples killed. But without civil war, the Patriarch will live to be a grand age, and perhaps have the love and daughters he deserves.

¶He is alive and with us now and is nine years old. His name is T***** M*****. And because of the war he will be wrongfully executed by firing squad. This will occur thirty two days after the war ends. And seventeen days later he will be pardoned by the new president, but it shall be too late. And these events will come to pass as they are here written.

¶We can not save him, for only life and the love of a woman can accomplish that task. In fact all there is to know is that he is a southern boy, and if he is executed as has been seen in the vision, we will be lost for almost a hundred years. For if he is executed it will mean that the northern armies have won the war. So we pray that if there must be war, that the south prevails over the north, that the Patriarch will live. Though we would have a divided Union, it would be for the good of all.

¶This will be the war of all wars, with more death and destruction than all to follow. And the aftermath will be terrible to behold, for it will serve only one purpose, to preserve the Union, which in another vision would come together by compromise and choice in thirty years, without bloodshed and destruction. Which would prevent the deaths of the Princesses of the bloodline, as well as turn the British monarchy into a republick. Thus the north must not win this war at any cost.

¶And with the death of the Patriarch, we will all fall melancholy, knowing that not one of us can do anything save for live and preserve the bloodline and teach our children to carry on our ways until the Patriarch is born in the next century and seek him out.

¶He shall be reborn inside a hundred years from now. And on the anniversary of the great war, he will feel a kinship with it, but know not why. And within the war he will live both to its study and era. And he will be approximately the age he is now as T** M*****, for he will be T** M***** in all respects, from his appearance to his nature.

¶He will appear as if he is out from time, both dressing and acting as T** does now. And in many ways he will preserve the great war, and carry it with him through life. And none will understand.

¶And when it leaves him, he will become lost, as he will lose T** at the same age T** will die. For here is sadness, for he will want to stay as the disposition and good nature of T**, but the spirit of T** will leave him, and he will become empty and full with sorrow.

¶Yet during the time he will spend with the spirit of T** he will be content, yet know he is empty. And when T** leaves, he will be as the dead who walk, knowing only meloncholia and despair.

¶He will be an outcast, knowing there is a purpose, but also knowing there is no answer. And he will walk alone, unloved.

¶There are always two sides to a vision of prophesy, and it is the events which come to pass that choose which one will be etched in time. His is not yet etched in the ages. But I shall shew you both as they come to me in the stone.

¶Both shew a life of sadness and despair. Yet of superior intellect as well as skill and talent. Both shew a man of great potential of love, but who is unloved. Both shew a man of great capacity for giving knowledge and understanding, yet not being understood.

¶Both visions are much clouded by events which will or will not be. Each one mutable by its surrounding events, yet each starts the same but comes to two different ends.

¶In the one vision, he is placed into a grave, marked only by a tombstone engraved by himself with the terrible words "unloved and unwanted", yet there are several women at the gravesite who lament, crying, "Why is this so, should I have known this outcome, I would have thrown myself into his arms at any cost and given my love freely, why had I not done this while he lived". And all will be lost.

¶In the second vision, she who was chosen by him, but would not love him will, as a seer, experience the first vision and knowing it to be true, will act upon it and prevent its outcome. She will submit and give her love to him as she will realize the importance of the matter.

¶And here, others will follow, and three daughters will be

born to him by three different women. And thus, Lilith will feel the first stab of pain in her black and shriveled heart and will begin to die.

¶And so, sons and daughters of Arcadia, these are my prophesies on this matter. Mark them well and watch for signs and omens and teach your children to watch also. For we are in the last days of our race, and the future is not yet written, thus we can have a hand in which version is to be read.

Our Dispensations and Dispositions

¶First amongst all of Arcadia is the Patriarch, for he is the incarnation of all of our blood. And though we may live without him living amongst us, it is our duty to prepare for him that he shall meet her who will set him free from his curse and save us.

¶Know the Patriarch by his blood mark. He above all is the oldest of the Merovingians, and will display many talents and dispensations, and know things to mastery which have not been taught to him.

¶And he is darkest of us with great despair and melancholia. And he, being pure of the bloodline, has the blood of all Arcadians running through his veins. And through his blood we can live again, as he can impart our ancestry unto us through the blood rite.

¶His talents and dispositions are greatest. His sorrow and sadness is greatest. His despair and meloncholia is greatest. His love and devotion to the bloodline and its people is greatest.

¶He may go anywhere in the world openly and live, but he lives the life of the dead, for he has never been loved. But by his knowledge and wisdom and talents he can be many people, yet always himself. For he remembers all aspects of lives past and needs no education to be able to work and live.

¶He is the sacrificer of his own happiness for that of others of the bloodline. His strength is great, his understanding is great and his lust is great, but can only sire a female child with she who is truly loving and also old of Arcadia. He is without age while he is vital, he is ancient when his ethers are being tapped by strife.

¶During some ages he is known unto us, during other ages we know of him, but he knows not of us, yet he does know of us yet we only exist in his instincts.

¶He also possesses certain items, being an amulet which shews us that he is the Patriarch, 2 seer stones of which one is white with notches cut around the edges and a hole in the centre and the other being brown and oblong with blue speckeling and a hole in the centre. He also possesses other items some of which are small gold bees.

¶His appearance is that of a man out of time, as is his disposition, for he is capturing the time previous to his present life, for that is his instinct. And as he is of all time, this be how he shews his nature.

¶Take care not to alert him to his duty or dispensations, yet if you ever come upon him and suspect him of being our Patriarch take much care to discover if he is the man who is shewn here. For if he is, and you bring him home to us you shall be ten fold blessed amongst Arcadia.

¶Approach him carefully in order to determine if he is the Patriarch. In no wise alert him to our ways, for we must discover him, and he must discover us, and each and every aspect of his being must be confirmed as set down here.

¶He craves to preserve the Grail, but knows this not, yet will his cravings and all else which defines him become instinct unto him. And though he knows not that it is Grail he craves, he shall have an instinct to seek constantly, for it is the bloodline of the Yaernessa (Pure and Divine Princesses) he craves.

¶If you approach him blindly and with jubilation he will shun you and not believe you. It is also possible that you could awaken him too fast and bring upon his memory of incarnations past and he will shun you out of confusion.

¶For though he is first amongst us, and our strength, his soul and heart is as glass.

¶Understand his disposition should you discover him. Know that by his actions he is stern and strict yet kind and gentle, yet within he feels pain which you could never imagine and this is hidden from you, for he has lived a thousand lifetimes in lonliness and without love.

¶There are times when we all walk together, as now. And there are times when we walk in tribes only having contact through the Elders. And there are times when we walk together with the Patriarch.

¶Yet all may not know the Patriarch, for this is not the right of the newly initiated Yaernasa or Yaernes. But is the right of the families and Elders and Protectors.

¶It is the greatest honour to become of the bloodline of the Patriarch and for him to offer it, for then he may share his wisdom, knowledge and powers with you, and you will be the better for it. And you will then be more than a generation old, you will be brought to your age of incarnation and start to remember.

¶Only by decree of the Patriarch can a man or woman be brought into the bloodline by the Graal Rite. If the Patriarch is hidden to us, or has not incarnated or is not of age, the Elders may elect and have the authority to bring someone into the bloodline.

¶It is the duty of the Patriarch to give prophesie to the Royal Houses. He will also guide us when we are being attacked by our enemies, and all will heed his instruction, that we may survive their wrath.

¶And he will know whom amongst people are worthy to come into the bloodline. And in his presence, you will not be able to act falsely, for he will cause you to shew your real self to him and others around him. By this talent know him well. For if you be false or evil you will reveal yourself as such. Likewise if you are true and good, you will shew these qualities.

¶And if you have a certaine talent, he will manifest it to its fullest in you. And with him you will shew all who you are and were in past incarnations, for you are in the presence of ancient blood.

The Elders

¶There be five kinds of Elders which serve the Royal Houses. Each has his own Dispensation and Purpose unto our kind, for our kind. And they be Major Elders, Minor Elders, Greater Elders, Lesser Elders and Appointed or Chosen Elders.

Major Elders

¶Major Elders are direct family bloodline. They are the families by which the bloodline is carried on through marriage and the lineage of descent.

¶These are the ancient families of the Arcadia. They hold rule over the Elders under them, and will rule and hold Council with all other Elders when the Patriarch is not born.

¶And the oldest and wisest patriarch of these families will give the Prophesies and guide and keep the families together.

Minor Elders

¶They are the natural born children of the Major Elders. They are able by their lineage to carry on the bloodline. Yet the men and women of these families must only marry into the bloodline or from Chosen or Appointed Elders, which the Patriarch brings into the bloodline.

¶It is the duty of the Minor Elders to seek out those who would be Appointed or Chosen by the Patriarch. It is also their duty to find his mates in order to continue the bloodline and lineage.

¶The Patriarch may take his mates from the Major, Minor or Chosen and Appointed Elders Houses.

¶And there will be always one who is a Minor Elder who will befriend the Patriarch and advise him as a friend and advisor of the Bloodline.

¶Be warned and know well that it is the first families of the Minor Elders who will be most looked upon and regarded as being Arcadian. Thus, be warned that you serve to be recognized to the Patriarch for what you are.

¶And though they may not know they are of the Bloodline in some cases, they will have the instinct to Quest for the Grail with their chosen mates.

Greater Elders

¶They be the children by bloodline of the Minor Elders. Their service is unto the Bloodline. Yet some may fall away from our kind, only to have their children or children's children come back to us.

Lesser Elders

¶They be the mates chosen by the Greater Elders to marry into the Bloodline. It is from here that the Bloodline grows thin, and they must return to the Patriarch and the Major Elders to replenish their strength.

¶Know that this is your line of succession and from where you descend. Know also that for centuries our peoples have inhabited certain lands such as France, Scotland, Ireland, Poland, Prussia, Austria and Bavaria. And now we inhabit

America, as here will be the final battle be fought.

Chosen or Appointed Elders

¶Chosen or Appointed Elders are taken from the families. They are those who have had many incarnations and know full well the Bloodline and are ancient by the blood of Wisdom and Knowledge, and were there when the curse was wrought upon our kind.

¶And though the Patriarch knows them, he will reveal naught unto them, for they must discover their purpose alone, and reveal it unto him.

¶Yet he will know them upon sight, and their families. Yet he will observe their ability to understand and remember.

Protectors

¶They are chosen from all the Elders. It is their sworn duty to see that the Patriarch is not murdered or harmed. They also swear to protect him from meloncholia.

¶They are gentle unto him and do not readily reveal themselves unto him. Yet they must question him by these ways to determine if he is in fact the Patriarch. For if they choose to protect the wrong man, Lilith is close and waiting. (ed.note- This applies to the search for the Patriarch, when he is not amongst. Fortunately we have found our Patriarch many years ago).

> "Gather, ye Protectors, when the time of reckoning draws nigh. And protect thy Patriarch, that he lives in the time of reckoning and does not take his own life from despair.
>
> Guide him well, and take heed the words of the prophesies. Mate him well or all thy blood will boil for an eternity by the fire and smoke of Lilith. And we will all be lost, and it will all have been for naught."
>
> *Book of Sorrows.*

¶It is also the duty of the Protectors to watch and report to the Council of Elders any dangers to our kind.

¶There are also those of the Protectors caste who are called the Watchers. It is their duty to seek out those who are of Arcadia, through bloodline and incarnation and seek the Graal Rite.

¶Upon knowing and finding and discovering them to be of Arcadia by incarnation, and having memories of our way and kind, the Watchers will make a study of them.

¶And should they truly have the Instinct, they may be brought amongst us, that we may study them. And they shall be judged either to be of us, or not of us by the Council of Elders.

¶And if they truly have the Memory and Instinct, they may be brought home amongst us by decree of the Patriarch. And they may be brought home amongst the Generations by the Blood Rite.

The Generations

Lesser Generations

¶The Lesser Generations are brought into the Bloodline by the Lesser and Greater Elders. This is done by the Lesser Blood Rite.

¶Those who are chosen to be Lesser Generations, have not been part of us before by incarnation. This is their first time, and from this time on they may incarnate into the bloodline if they prove themselves.

¶Lesser Generations can not generate a bloodline.

Greater Generations

¶The Greater Generations are those who have been lost from

us, yet who have instinct to our ways. They are brought into the bloodline by the Minor Elders.

¶They have had incarnations in the Bloodline, and wish to return.

¶They be brought back through the Greater Graal Rite. Yet they can not sire our kind, save they marry into a house of Minor Elders, and here, will only sire children of a Lesser or Greater house, save if they sire children who have had many incarnations as Arcadians.

¶Yet alone they can not sire a Bloodline with their own generation.

Minor Generations

¶The Minor Generations know they are Arcadian, yet were not born to a family of the Bloodline. Yet they know us by nature, instinct and incarnation, and even may practice the Grail Rites with their mates.

¶Upon marriage with their own generation, they may sire children of a house fit to be called Greater Elders.

¶Yet if their first child is a son, they will be fit only to be a house of the Lesser Elders.

Major Generations

¶Those who are the Major Generations seek us out and know us upon sight. They have had many incarnations and know us well.

¶Many of them come from families who have the bloodline, yet who have forgotten the ways of our ancient race.

¶When those of the Major Generations return home, and take the Major Graal Rite, they will start to remember and bring the knowledge, wisdom and instincts of their incarnations from the past unto the present.

¶And when they marry of their generation, they will have a house of Greater Elders. And should they have as their first child a daughter, and sire more daughters than sons, they will be cast as Minor Elders. And thus be the manner of comming into our fold.

The Councils of Arcadia

High Council

¶The Houses of Arcadia have always been governed by Councils, that our ways may be preserved, and our peoples kept safe.

¶The High Council are the Elders who sit below the Patriarch, or act in his place if he is not born, or is too young to guide us.

¶The duty of this Council is to keep accurate records of our families and the Partiarchs, Princes and Princesses.

¶They will also make our laws, which none but the Patriarch may change if he sees fit. They shall also raise houses by rank and degree.

¶They Shall make decisions concerning they who would become Generations as well as they who would be watched by us for signs that they are of Arcadia.

¶Only by their permission can the Graal Rites be performed and sanctioned. It is also this council which has the power to Banish any person who has broken faith with our ways. And it is they who will hold court over them.

¶The High Council is appointed by the Patriarch from the oldest houses. Yet, all lesser patriarchs of each house with his mates, may sit on this council and have a vote, in any of its matters and business. And if the Patriarch is not born nor found nor old enough to sit in the head chair, the patriarchs and their mates from each house of the Major Elders will conduct the council.

¶And the High council will be concerned with all the houses of all Elders, no matter their rank or degree, and help and advise them, as they would have done unto themselves.

Lesser Council

¶They shall have the duty of settling disputes of family and territory, and keeping a watchful eye on the generations, lest they stray from our ways.

¶They shall make sure that all of the houses, whether Major, Minor, Greater or Lesser, act in harmony with each other and help each other as they feel the need to be helped. And none will ever go without.

¶They will have the duty of seeking the Yaernessa (*Princesses, ed.*) who would mate with the Patriarch, and give him daughters so Lilith can be defeated.

¶They will also appoint those who will seek out the Yaernessa. Which is a great honour, as here respect for wisdom and devotion of the bloodline is celebrated.

¶And they shall appoint Protectors of the bloodline, and all those who fight for it and devote themselves to it.

¶And they will look for signs of Lilith and report them to this Council, that we may fight the demoness who plagues us. And by knowledge of her infernal ways, we will thwart her every move.

Council of Advisors

¶The Advisors are chosen from the houses of the families, each for their particular talent, knowledge and wisdom regarding any circumstance which affects our ways and existence.

¶This Council may change, or it may stand as is needed. It must be approved by the High Council and each appointed member, be they male or female must shew and display their divers talents and skills to the High Council, before they are approved.

¶Each Advisor shall act within his element and not outside of it. And to their element shall they only advise with wisdom and knowledge.

¶And their council will be wise and gentle and given with compassion, care and knowledge for the good of all.

The Bloodline

¶Our family bloodline is long and ancient. We are many by incarnation and few by direct bloodline of family lineage. Yet we are strong and will not be overcome by the evils wrought by Lilith.

¶We come through the bloodline by our houses and families, and are of the blood just as divers races are of their race and can not change their appearance.

¶It is natural for us to incarnate together in families, that we may be together. Know that by both incarnation and bloodline you will be strongest and first amongst Arcadians.

¶Know also that you can be of the bloodline of the families, yet be young by incarnation.

¶Know that many of us are strong by our incarnations, yet we be separated according to family.

¶And here, know that the Graal Rite can bring you back to the fold, and you will know your family and position therein.

¶And by incarnation, you will know Arcadia through instinct and nature. Thus you will never be lost from your own kind.

¶Yet many will have to await the Awakening, where they will have the instinct to return in full and to remember the past.

¶And in the Time of Reckoning they will band together by instinct, drawn to each other to kill the demoness Lilith, and to thwart her deeds of evil.

¶And many will come home to the fold at this time to fight her. And they will come home by the blood which sustains us, and through the generations.

¶And with those of us who have remained strong, they will regard us as their rightful families, as they will know our souls as their own. For as a family, we be stronger and more steadfast than even their birth families.

¶And know full well that in those times there will be agents of Lilith who will try and become family with us, though they be our enemies.

¶Know that many must be shunned and not allowed to go within our kind or our families. And we must hide ourselves from them, as they carry the evil of Lilith.

¶Use your instincts well, on who will walk with us. Know that by prophesie that many peoples may not walk with us or become part of our clan. That they serve Lilith and must be shunned, even in friendship. For she will use their weak wills and poison their blood.

¶Know also that because they do not follow the natural order of man and woman, that they can not accept the blood. And also know they are marked by Lilith and are of her kind and must be shunned.

¶And none who serve the ways of Lilith may be permitted to become of the generations, and could never be of the bloodline.

¶We have shewn the manner by which the generations are brought into our fold. Know also that generations may be brought into the families to become part of that family. Know that here, by special dispensation of the Patriarch, generations may become wives, daughters, husbands and sons, as a house requires.

The Grail Rites

¶Know that the purpose of the Grail Rites is three fold. In the first matter our wisdom is passed through the sacred allegories of the Sang Graal, that we may be strong as one made up of many that we may be protected from Lilith and fight her.

¶Know also that through the Grail Rites, we become stronger together. Know that the Graal Rites allow us to remember the strengths of our incarnations that we may preserve the knowledge, wisdom and experiences of our other lives.

¶Know that in the third matter, by way of the Graal Rites we may preserve and become pure and strong within our very souls. And may know things which were learned in the past, yet never taught us in the present.

¶Know that when you accept the Lineage of your ancients, you will become stronger in mind, spirit and body. And you will be able to overcome evil. And wisdom and knowledge may be passed from one to another such as a Major Elder can pass to a Lesser Elder that he may take as a wife.

¶For all memory, lineage, wisdom, knowledge and experience is contained in the allegory of the Grail Rites. And the wisdom of the ancients collects such virtues through the Lineage as the families continue.

¶And this can be passed on by family bloodline. Or it can be imparted through the Grail Rites.

¶And knowledge of these secrets, has had us cast out from the world and has had us marked as outcasts.

¶Though our purpose is good, Lilith has even invaded the minds of the church and other superstitious doctrines to mark us as evil, for our knowledge is dangerous to the church and it's truth concerning the crucifixion could destroy their doctrine and dogma.

¶Know well that our Lineage is ancient and sanctioned by

the first creator and his consort. And we have special dispensations and strengths which others have naught.

¶That one of the Minor or Major Elders is proficient in a talent, and a Lesser or Greater Elder is not, the virtues of the proficient Elder can be given to he who is without the talent, and he shall have it imparted unto him by the Grail Rites.

¶That also by our strength of the Grail, we may know each other's thoughts and thus be aware of when we are needed by the other. Many of us have the abilitie to communicate by thought alone.

¶Even they who are born deaf, blind and dumb may communicate if they have accepted the Lineage. For we are the Chosen Peoples who by the will of the Architect and his consort, Yse, must overcome Lilith and Lucifer and restore order to this world.

¶For here is our purpose and dispensation. And thereby we swear our allegience to this task.

¶There be many Grail Rites. Each to a specifick purpose. And many are known and held only in the ancient writings which are well guarded by the Pactio Secreta.

¶And there be a Grail Rite for healing, long life, against disease, talents, wisdom, skills, detecting agents of Lilith, to repel aging, strength, remembering incarnations, to know your purpose, to inspire love, to inspire lust and for bringing in generations & etc.

¶Know that for any purpose of excellence or protection there is a Grail Rite. Know also that when the Lineage is passed, they who receive it shall also receive its lineage, strength and power only to the level of the understanding of their incarnations and position in the Lineage.

¶And the level of lineage & etc. that will be received depends upon the House of he who imparts the Lineage. As a Major Elder who imparts the Lineage to a Minor Elder will create greatness in the Minor Elder to his abilitie. A Lesser

Elder who imparts the Lineage to a generation will increase the abilitie of the generation.

¶That the Lineage imparted to a Greater Generation by a Major Elder will make the Greater Generation more potent in his abilitie and understanding and rememberance, than if the Lineage was imparted unto him by a Greater Elder.

¶Thusly both the imparting and receiving of the Lineage is proportional to the Position of the giver and the receiver.

¶The greater the Position of he who imparts the Lineage, the greater the dispensations bestowed upon he who receives the Lineage.

¶The greater the Position of he who has the Lineage imparted unto him, the greater will be the power which is bestowed upon him.

¶Know that the passing of the Lineage must always be from male to female or female to male. It must never be passed from male to male, save for those who are brothers of the clan, and this must be done through a female.

¶Princesses of the clan may pass the blood from one to another with a Prince, betwixt them, and he will be the better for it.

¶The Lineage may be passed to those who are young to remember their past knowledge. We choose for the young to grow to discover for themselves if they hear the calling. When it has been decided by the High Council that they do remember and have the instinct, they may take the Graal Rite accordyng to their needs.

¶Know well that when the Lineage is passed, you will aquire virtues from he who passes it to you. In this wise, know that you can partake of divers virtues and qualities.

¶The Graal Rite must be repeated until you have developed the virtues and qualities naturally within your self.

Passing the Lineage

¶There are divers times to pass the Lineage, which must be honoured. And also there is a specifick manner in which the Graal Rite is performed.

¶When you wish to perform the ritual for a specifick purpose, you must consult with the patriarch of your house and then the High Council, that they may prepare the Rite. For without the preparation ritual, you will affect naught.

¶And those who are ill or afflicted with any sickness or disease must never pass their lineage until they are healed.

¶The times for passing the Lineage must be observed diligently. The Lineage must never be passed during the darkness of the moon. The best time is during the fullness of the moon.

¶The Bloodline of the Arcadians is ancient blood and as precious as gold, and thus must not be wasted on those who are not worthy.

¶Thus, you will be given signs, that you know who is worthy to accept the Lineage. That there be signs given by both men and women, and without these signs you must refrain from the performing the Graal Rite.

¶Know that, you may see who is bloodline or who is to be generations by the eyes and their manner and disposition. And the talk of Arcadia fills them with inspiration and illumination.

¶And should she be overcome with the hysteria of passion, she will show a great and wonderful sign which cannot be false in its manner.

¶That a sign be that she will feel greatly passionate and loving, and become of her true nature without care for her actions. She will become very passionate and overcome with emotion, and she will show the sign of her office without care, in this action and not try to avoid it and this will make her feel complete.

¶And if she displays herself in this manner, she is truly a Princess of Arcadia and has come home. And she will be regarded as a Yaernessa. Know this by the sign that she shall spill her living waters upon the earth.

¶But if the evil of Lilith should interfere with her feelings at this time, and cause her to hide these signs, she is not worthy of Arcadia, and will be reduced to a shriveled hag. For then she is of fire and not water, and shall be shunned and cast out.

¶And water be the manner of females who are Yaeras who be special and can help defeat the evil of Lilith. And they above all are most important to us and are held higher than the rest in importance to our race and purpose. For only they can save our race from extinction.

¶And they, both male and female will feel as a family with those who are of Arcadia, who have instinct and memory of their incarnations..

¶And in the presence of the Patriarch, those females who have the instinct and memory will desire his Lineage if they are among the most ancient and special and recognize him, and in his presence shall spill their living waters to the earth.

¶And they will feel complete inside their souls in his presence. And he will cause them to reveal their true nature of living water, and love them.

¶Yet know that those women who would love him, also feel that he is above them, and may not pursue his love. And they may be of the generations, and feel that they must not go to him. And this is his curse and the reason he is stronger and above us. For unto him, there is only melancholia and despair, and he knows that he is unworthy of the love and happiness which is so common to the rest of us. For he is the Fisher King and only she who will give him the Chosen Response at his kiss, will break the Curse on the Grail Family. And she is of water, and not fire.

¶Yet any woman who recognizes him and desires as well as craves his Lineage, and thinks of him lovingly is special. And should she overcome the ways and manner of publick society and embrace him, she will be stronger than Lilith and overcome her.

¶And the stronger her love and passion for him, and the more women which are as her, who do the same, the more chance we shall have of overcomming Lilith and her evil.

¶Yet if she does not crave his Lineage and become water at the thought of him or his embrace and kiss of fire, or if she avoids him because he may be with another, she is untrue and not of Arcadia, but perhaps of Lilith or of the common publick society with no bloodline or lineage.

¶Know that at certaine times, men will be appointed Princes of Arcadia, and their duty is high and important to us. And though they may not be of the High Elders, and maybe even of the Greater generations, by decree of the High Council or of the Patriarch, they will be given the position of Prince.

¶This position is extremely important to all Arcadians, as here, he who is appointed is held high in trust and council as an advisor and also a seeker of they who will restore us, by defeating Lilith.

¶And they who are made Princesses by decree, may discover their true nature in the same way as does a Prince.

¶Know that the love of a Prince and Princess is great, yet it is not as great as a Princess and the Patriarch. For they cannot generate the Bloodline, though they be appointed, save if they are of the Major Elders.

¶And the Princesses who seek the Patriarch by instinct as he seeks them are doubly blessed against the wrath of Lilith and her evil hoarde. And their love is blessed ten fold.

¶Know that a Prince may be appointed, yet a Princess appointed is not as great as a Princess who is natural by her disposition of water.

¶And the Bloodline of a Princess shared with a Prince creates a great power which can help our people, by protecting the Bloodline. As they can find the Princesses who will preserve the Bloodline.

¶Know that the riddle is great, and our goal is high. Know that it is the most difficult goal to reach, and if it can be reached and overcome, all else can be overcome.

¶Know that the Patriarch is always hidden to all but the Major Elders. And he, himself, may not even know that he serves us and is our figurehead. Thus we must always be aware of the signs which reveal him. And his discovery is a difficult task.

¶And to find those Princesses who will give him love is a more difficult task. Yet if they be found, his meloncholia and despair will cease, and thus will we also shed our despair.

¶Yet even they may believe he is beyond their approach, and they are unworthy of him. But think ye not his. As his is a wretched lot, of strife, meloncholia and despair, and he who is the Patriarch, would feel unworthy of the Love.

¶And he walks alone by night, and knows nothing but darkness and her sadness. And he lives inside himself, never revealing himself, that he would rather suffer, than gamble and bargain for that which would save his soul.

¶For he is the outcast of outcasts, alone, cold and tired. And would not know the Love even if he were to see it, for he has no way of knowing it, save for the sign of the living waters.

¶And those Princesses who are true, will shew their signs and thus reveal themselves. And should they ever fall to love the Patriarch, they will know an ecstacy within their veins and hearts which will move them to great desire.

¶And if such greatness in women ever be found, they will be taken aside and prepared, that they may present themselves to the Patriarch, duly and truly prepared as their station demands.

¶And they shall even love each other though they be Princesses, for their love and desire be great.

¶This love will be great and powerful, and the desire will be more true than among mortal men and women. For here, the desire and devotion shall be as never seen before. And should it come to pass, we shall all revel in its beauty.

¶For even unto the Lesser Elders, the Appointed and the Chosen the Love of the Merovingian Arcadian is greater than that of the mortal, and its devotion goes beyond the grave.

¶Yet, cursed is she who knows that her lot is to seek the Patriarch, yet who avoids him. For she will dry up inside and wither as a hag.

¶And her beauty will fade. And she will grow old and sick and sad and suckle his despair. And she will find no happiness, for she will have forsaken it.

of the Divers Grail Rites and the Manner in which they should be Conducted

¶Know that there are divers Grail Rites for each purpose unto our ways and customs. And they must be carried out exactly as shewn. For if they are not, the blood will be wasted.

The Major Rite

¶The Major Rite is the most important of all our rituals and ceremonies. It can only be performed by a First Elder and a Princess. Though it be better and more complete if it is performed by the Patriarch and his Princesses.

¶The High Council must approve the candidate for this rite, before it can be granted.

¶The purpose of this rite is to make a Major Elder, Seal friends and lovers, to receive the ancestral Lineage, to make

Princes and Princesses..

¶This Rite also includes the Grand Rite, which is the Sacred Marriage Rite. This Rite can only be performed by the Patriarch and his Princesses or the First elder and his Princess or a Chosen and Appointed Prince and Princess who belong to a house of Major Elders. For it is the most sacred of all our rites, and only by it can a house be raised.

Minor Rite

¶This rite is used to remember and know divers talents and skills which you have known in past incarnations, that you may know them now in the present. It be also used to gain greater wisdom and knowledge of things which you know and would desire to know better. That a tailor may become a better tailor, a captain may become a better captain &etc.

¶This rite also must be performed by Major Elders, or duly and truly Chosen and Appointed Princes and Princesses.

Greater Rite

¶This rite is used to bind and seal lovers and to heal and impart knowledge and lineage. It may be performed by Minor Elders and Chosen and Appointed Princes and Princesses.

Lesser Rite

¶This Rite is used to make generations, both lesser and greater. And this is only done through the blood of the Major Elders, Minor Elders or Chosen and Appointed Elders being Princes and Princesses.

The Affirmation

¶This rite is performed by the clan once each season unto their own houses. And each who is above, giving blood to each who is below in celebration of our race and our houses.

¶This celebration is marked by a feast, and is a sacred time for us to perform the Rites as needed. Each celebration is overseen by a Prince and Princess, who conduct the rites accordynge to our ancient traditions and customs.

The Bloodline Rites

¶The particulars of our Grail Rites are written down in our sacred record and kept by the Scribes of the First House of Elders and overseen by the First Elder or the Patriarch.

¶And they must only be read or performed accordynge to the position of those unto whom the rites favour. For one may not know that which is not of their station.

The Love and Sacred Wedding of the Arcadians

¶The Love of a man and woman in our ancient race is more true than that of men and women of the common publick.

¶And that love is even deep when we find and choose our mates from outside our race and bring them home unto our clan.

¶And that love must never be violated, even by thought and desire of another, once it is proclaimed. For if this comes to pass, ruination and damnation and death will come to he who cherishes she who is chosen and taken.

¶And this violation shall be visited unto the family of the violators, even that those who avenge the love will be hanged for their revenge it shall be done.

¶Know that, when a woman is chosen and taken by one of Arcadia, she is his. And he who desires her shall die a horrible death, as will his family and any who help him interfere with the Love.

¶And any who are truly Merovingian/Arcadian, and who feel any desire for she who is taken, will swiftly change their ways and think no longer of she who is chosen and taken.

¶For we are above the common publick, and do not desire any woman who is taken within our Houses. For the penalty is death.

¶And even if she feels this way, she shall kill these feelings within herself. And only by consent of her mate shall she be let go. And even then, the High Council shall judge this action by Sacred Decree.

The Sacred Wedding

¶We have two forms of marriage. The first is the Lesser Wedding, which lasts for All Time, being the lifetime of the bride and groom.

¶The second is the Greater Wedding, which lasts for All Time and Eternity, being for all incarnations.

¶Both are marked by a Sacred Ring. Which in the case of the Greater Wedding is made of gold with golden spurs on the inside, which may be slid onto the finger, but never pulled off without ripping the flesh off of the finger.

¶There shall be one spur for each degree of houses accordynge to their importance.

¶The inscription on the ring will read, 'For All Time And Eternity', with a skull and crossbones at the centre. Within the ring shall be the name of the bride and groom.

¶The ring for the Lesser Wedding, shall have the arms of

the house engraved thereon, and have no spurs within.

¶The names of the bride and groom will be engraved within the ring.

Concernynge Princes and Princesses

¶Princes and Princesses of the Merovingians, are the first chosen amongst the families of the Minor and Major houses. And it is only they who may perform our Sacred Rituals, and perform the Blessings & etc.

¶It is the Prince who raises the power in the Princess and directs it to do the work of the ritual.

¶The Princes and Princesses are natural to their positions, and thereby are chosen for their virtues and qualities.

¶That of the Princess is most important, yet she must have a Prince to guide and protect her. It is the Princesses who have the power to fight the demoness Lilith.

¶Thusly, each Princess must be duly and truly consecrated and taught the ways of the Princess, which are never revealed to any other women of Arcadia, save they who discover the secret, or discussed by the men of Arcadia.

¶The Princess is Consecrated to her duty and ritually prepared by other Princesses only, and no man, save for the Patriarch may ever know the ritual.

¶Her body and mind is cleansed and dedicated to fighting Lilith that she may be her direct opposite, and thus protect herself from the evil which Lilith can manifest.

¶And each Princess has the right to take another Princess as a companion that they may be sealed and become stronger against Lilith.

¶And those females who have an instinct to love one another are readily chosen as Princesses. But they must not stray from the Prince which they are bound to, unless he willingly gives them unto another Prince, and they accept this act of love.

¶And only a Prince may be Sealed to a Princess, and no Princess may be Sealed unto he who is not a Prince. And a Prince may be Sealed to more than one Princess, that he may have many Princesses as spiritual mates.

¶And the greater the Prince, the more Princesses he may have as mates, so long as it is sanctioned by the Patriarch or First Elder.

¶And Great is the Prince, who discovers the Patriarch and presents him with a Princess, or gives up one of his Princesses, that the Patriarch may find the Sacred Love.

¶And greater is she, who is a Princess, who embraces and loves the Patriarch for she shalt be eternally blessed and loved and protected.

¶And there be divers degrees of Princes and Princesses. That some be lesser, greater, minor and major. And some be above Major and be pure Yaernessa.

¶And each degree of Princess is known to other Princesses by how she is prepared in body and mind.

¶All Princesses are known by their body decoration which is in the form of golden rings set into her body in divers places.

¶And the setting of rings determines her degree as a Princess. And the setting of Rings can only be done by the Patriarch or High Princesses.

¶And her body shall be shaven at all times to shew that she is opposite to Lilith who is the evil and hairy night fiend of Hell.

¶And she shall wear certaine types of clothing which shall show to other Yaeras, who she is, that they shall know her.

¶And she shall have certaine habits which shall also shew her as a Princess. And these habits shall embrace and celebrate her virtues, that we may know her as special amongst us.

¶And she is ageless, and will be as a woman child, and never lose her girlish ways nor grow old. And here, her youth and beauty is preserved. Yet she is as Yse, Sacred Goddess.

¶And the love of a Princess for another Princess is profound and deep. Yet she must never choose only females to love. She must have a Prince.

¶And she who is a Princess, by any degree, will know her Prince as him whose Bloodline she desires. And here shalt be their bond, even though she may only be a Princess by instinct, and not yet consecrated.

¶And a true Prince shall at times not pursue a Princess whom he loves, but let her choose him, that he shall be confirmed of that love.

¶And a true Princess will know her Prince by how she desires to protect him. And she will desire his Bloodline. And she will know his thoughts without words, but through his eyes.

¶And though he may recognize her, he will not try and court her. For she must choose him, though he may suffer.

Concernynge our Doctrine of Belief

¶The Merovingians have a doctrine and belief unlike any other peoples. Our doctrine defines us and sets us apart from others.

¶We are not a religious peoples in the Biblical sense of the multitude of religions who speak in terms of hellfire and brimstone.

¶We are a religious peoples in the sense of truth, being that we fight the evil which has plagued mankind.

¶We believe in the sanctity and preservation of our Bloodline and Lineage.

¶We believe in guarding the Patriarch and in seeking his

Princesses.

¶We believe that we must fight and overcome Lilith, that we may restore the Wasteland.

¶We believe that we are a separate race amongst the common publick, and we are their guardians against evil.

¶We believe that we were chosen as a peoples to fight the evils of Lilith.

¶We believe that we may pass on virtues, skills, abilities and remembrance of past incarnations by the Graal Rites.

¶We believe in Eternal Marriage and love between Prince and Princesses.

¶We believe in loyalty and honour amongst those who are Merovingian.

¶We believe that we are descended from the God and Goddess, who created mankind and are of them in image.

¶And as part of them, we feel no need to worship them in the common manner. But pay them homage by becomming as them, in their image.

¶We believe in seeking those who are as us through family Bloodline and incarnation, and watching for omens that they may recognize our ways and come home to us.

¶We believe in the prophesies which tell us of the future and how to fight Lilith.

¶We believe that we shall live many lives, incarnating again and again to accomplish this task.

¶We believe in seeking out Princesses to fight Lilith, and this is our duty and honour.

Divine Mathematics and Grail Theology

Of all religious faiths and esoteric paths, only the path of the Holy Grail possesses a system of Divine Mathematics which is used to prove the theology and doctrine of the Grail teachings. All which is true to the Holy Grail is subject to certain and specific mathematics inherent in the Grail doctrine.

For the sake of clarity, we must backtrack in order to qualify and clarify the basis of the above statement. Joseph of Arimathea, in the year 54AD, performed a Grail Ritual which put him in communion with the Neutral Angels who carried the Grail to Earth. Each Angel appeared to Joseph in turn and spoke to him of the time of the pre-existence, when there were only Gods and Goddesses, how the physical universe came to be, the direction of mankind, the purpose of life, laws which govern man, nature and the universe, the Luciferian Rebellions and the future etc.

Joseph copied this down in the writing of the Grail language and it was called The Book of the Holy Grail. In both the Lesser Book and Greater Book is contained the history of the Gods and mankind as relates to the Royal Quest. Within this book all question of life and death, God, Goddesses, wisdom, knowledge, reincarnation, the sexes, the races, good and evil etc. are answered. To the Grail peoples this is The Merovingian Bible.

The Book of the Holy Grail, as it reads, is timeless. It was copied by each Grand Master successor from Joseph to Adam in 1776, in the Grail language. At any given time, it was the Grand Master's book which was taught from, and only to those who had entered the Fifth Spiritual Degree, who could speak the Grail tongue.

The first English translation was created in 1776 in Virginia. But, the Grail language didn't translate well into English. After much deliberation, the Grail language was Americanized in 1787 and the first hand copy of the Book of the Holy Grail is used for teaching. In the book, interestingly, is the fact that this is predicted in the book itself, and the time frame is accurate.

The Grail Priesthood Lineage has undergone several changes, all predicted in the sacred writings of the Grail. The first Priesthood were the Guardians of the Great Secret, given to Adam at the beginning of time by the Neutral Angels. This Priesthood had the duty of guarding the mysteries of the preexistence and of performing Divine Ordinances for the followers. The Priesthood was of limited size and only included High Priests.

The second manifestation of the Priesthood came through Jeshua ben Jusef (Jesus, son of Joseph). He instituted the grouping of 13, being a High Priest and 12 disciples, or apprentice priests. He also included the first office of High Priestess. The third and final manifestation of the priesthood came when Joseph of Arimathea took his wife Mary, Jeshua the Teacher and wives Mary Magdala and Mary of Bethany to France to escape the political uprising against his son's teachings. From this manifestation the Priesthood became locked within a single family, thus the Royal Bloodline was born.

These five people became the five principals of the Royal priesthood, being High Priest, Summoner, Princess, High Priestess and Maiden. These positions are still used in the High Priesthood Hierarchy today.

Within the Priesthood one will find the beginnings of the mathematical formula. Such as each priesthood temple being made up of 13 people, being 5 members of the Priesthood Hierarchy, and 8 apprentice Priests and Priestesses. Thus the first matter equation here is 5+8=13.

There are also '3' Physical Degrees, '5' Spiritual Degrees and

'5' Royal Degrees, thus the equation reads 3+5+5=13. The formula of 355 13 sacred to Yse, Divine Goddess and wife of The Great Architect of the Universe.

All 'feminine' aspects of the Grail must contain this formula to be correct and applicable to the Grail. There are also two other formulas which compliment this one in determining what is correct and true in the feminine sense of Grail theology and doctrine.

The Divine Mathematics of the Holy Grail is a vast' yet simple system of equations and formulas which support Grail life, theology, doctrine and ritual.

It is based on the English alphabet in which each letter has a corresponding number from 1 to 5 which is repeated.

This system of alphabet/number correspondence hold all the keys and riddles to the Holy Grail. It proves the nature of her representatives, called Princesses. It also proves the Sacred Grail Rituals which protect the Grail and reveals its allegorically to the Illuminated.

The interesting and sometimes confusing element of this alpha-numeric correspondence is that it only applies to the English language. In fact it is specifically stated in The Book of the Holy Grail ,that the system of Divine Mathematics will not be totally revealed until the 'chosen people reach the chosen land'(America). And then the system will become clear. Thusly, today we have answer, predicted in The Book of the Holy Grail over 1,900 years ago written by Joseph of Arimathea, which apply 'today' to the Royal Quest.

This aspect of Grail theology demands a degree of illumination which goes beyond faith or belief, as it transcends time. More importantly it applies to the 'time' when the chosen people will migrate to the chosen land, and at this time the chosen language will manifest itself in the Holy Grail. And this will constitute a sing for the families of the Grail to unite.

The following will illustrate several Grail equations. First, understand that to arrive at the Grail Formulas, each letter of the alphabet is assigned a number. Secondly know that there are 5 Sacred numbers, being; 5, 8, 13, 17, 23.

A

	13		— 13 =	5+8 or	3+5+5
8		17	— 17 =	1+7=8	8
5		23	— 23 =	2+3=5	+5
					13

B

H	O	L	Y	G	R	A	I	L
2 +	2 +	4 +	5=13	1 +	4 +	1 +	3 +	4=13
	3	5	5		5	3	5	

3+5+5=13   5+3+5=13   13+13=26,   2+6=8

In the above formulas labeled 'B', you can see that the equation is 'hidden', which means that the equation must be 'discovered' and translated from the given numbers.

Thus in HOLY we have the corresponding numbers of 2245 which equal '13' and can be broken down to reveal 355 if we; Take the first '2' and add one to it from the second '2' , to arrive at '3'. Then take the remaining '1' from the second '2' and add it to the '4' to arrive at '5'. Then we simply add on the '4' of 'L' to arrive at '5', and we see the equation 355.

Divine Mathematics

Key

A	B	C	D	E
1	2	3	4	5
F	G	H	IJ	K
5	1	2	3	4
L	M	N	O	P
4	5	1	2	3
Q	R	S	T	U
3	4	5	1	2
V	W	X	Y	Z
2	3	4	5	1

First Equation

```
        13      — 13=5+8 or     3+5+5
    8       17  — 17=1+7=8        8
    5       23  — 23=2+3=5       +5
                                 ---
                                  13

H     O     L     Y          G     R     A     I     L
2  +  2  +  4  +  5=13       1  +  4  +  1  +  3  +  4=13
|     |     |     |          |     |     |           /
|_____|_____|     |          |_____|     |_____/_____|
      |     |     |                |        /        |
      3     5     5                5     3           5
```

Second Equation

a — A I R
1 + 3 + 4=8
(AIR has 3 letters)

b — W A T E R
3 + 1 + 1 + 5 + 4=14, 1+4=5
(Water has 5 letters)

c — E A R T H
5 + 1 + 4 + 1 + 2=13
(Earth has 5 letters)

d — F I R E
5 + 3 + 4 + 5=17
(Fire has 4 letters)

Third Equation

3 5 5 (+4) = 17 (see ERIS equation)

A	W	E	F
I	A	A	I
R	T	R	R
	E	T	E
	R	H	

The Five Prime Patterns

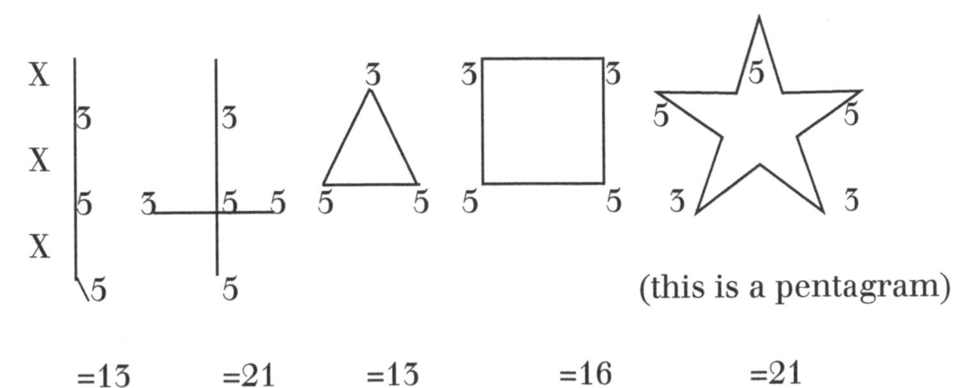

(this is a pentagram)

=13	=21	=13	=16	=21
=4	=3	=4	=7	=3

4 + 3 + 4 + 7 + 3

3 3 5 5 5

(this equation is arrived at by reduction and carrying)

First Explanatory Equation- A

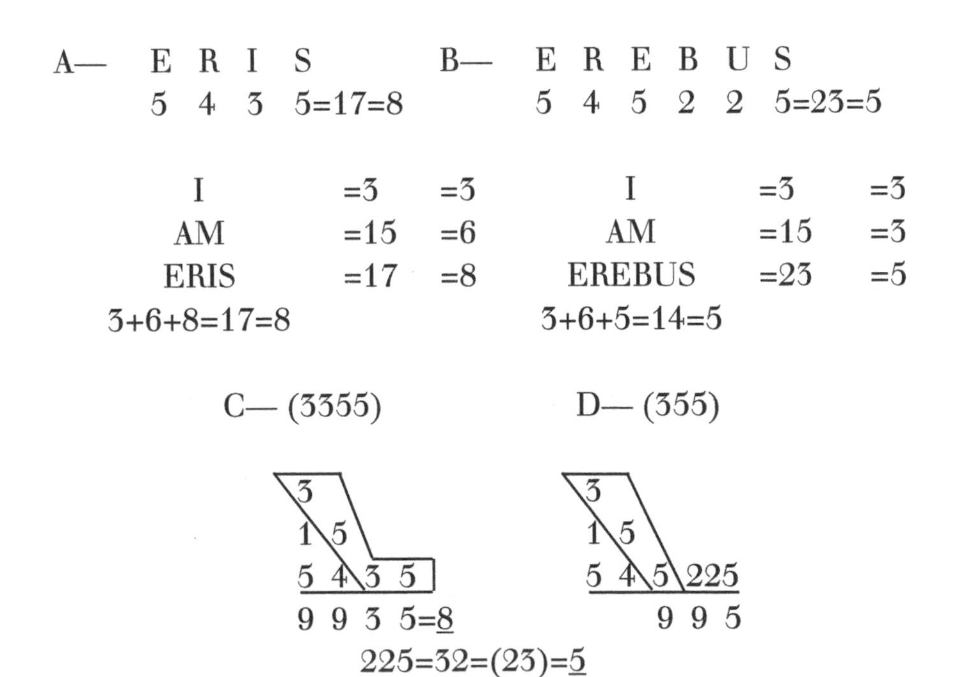

CONT.

A+C = 17+26 =43, 4+3 = 7

B+D = 14+32=46, 4+6 = +10, (1+0=1)

17

AC(7)+BD(1)=8

First Explanatory Equation-B

This formula shows how the Grail/Illuminati equations contain the 5 prime values of 5, 8, 13, 17, 23.

3 5 5 355=13, 355+13=26, 2+6=8

8 5 = 13 +2 +2= 17 355+1+3=17

\+ +

8 +5 + 13 +3 +3= 23

5 5

Angle equation 5+5+1+7+2+3=23

Right Angle Equation

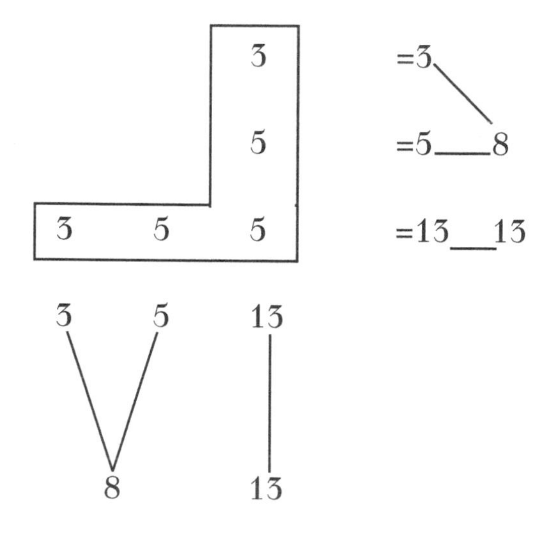

Feminine Words Containing the Grail Equation

P R I N C E S S
$\underline{3}$ 4 3 1 (3 5 5) $\underline{5}$ 355 3355 33555 (open and hidden)

P R I E S T E S S
$\underline{3}$ 4 (3 5 5) 1 $\underline{5}$ 5 5 355 3355 33 555 (open and hidden)

F E M I N I N E
5 $\underline{5}$ $\underline{5}$ $\underline{3}$ 1 $\underline{3}$ 1 $\underline{5}$ 355 3355 33555 (all hidden)

I N N O C E N C E
$\underline{3}$ 1 1 2 $\underline{3}$ $\underline{5}$ 1 3 $\underline{5}$ 355 3355 (hidden)

M A I D E N
$\underline{5}$ 1 $\underline{3}$ 4 $\underline{5}$ 1 355 (hidden)

S E N S I T I V E
$\underline{5}$ 5 1 $\underline{5}$ $\underline{3}$ 1 3 2 $\underline{5}$ 355 3355 33555 (all hidden)

A F F E C T I O N
1 $\underline{5}$ $\underline{5}$ $\underline{5}$ $\underline{3}$ 1 $\underline{3}$ 2 1 355 3355 33555 (all hidden)

P R E T T Y
$\underline{3}$ 4 $\underline{5}$ 1 1 $\underline{5}$ 355 (hidden)

S W E E T
5 (3 5 5) 1 355 (open)

P A S S I V E
$\underline{3}$ 1 $\underline{5}$ $\underline{5}$ $\underline{3}$ 2 $\underline{5}$ 355 3355 33555 (all hidden)

Intrinsic Words Containing the Grail Equation

Here are intrinsic words associated with the Holy Grail which contain the essential Grail Equations. Thusly, herein the words contain and hold the Grail 'secrets', and because of this, their association substantiates their relationship to the Holy Grail.

The first five words relate directly to the 'Philosophers Stone', which was said to have the virtues to turn 'base metals into pure gold'. Note that after the equations are removed from the words, the remainder equal the prime numbers of Grail/Illuminati doctrine.

Example 1, 2 & 3 are versions of the translation, 'stone from the heavens', or 'it fell from the heavens'.

1— L A P I S E X C A E L I S
4 1 3 3 5 5 4 3 1 5 4 3 5
3355 355
4+1 + 4 + 1 + 4+3=17

2— L A P S I T E X C A E L I S
4 1 3 5 5 1 5 4 3 1 5 4 3 5
355 355
4+1+ 5+1 + 4=15 1+ 4+3=8,15+8=23

3— L A P S I T E X C I L L I S
4 1 3 5 3 1 5 4 3 3 4 4 3 5
3355
4+1+ 5+ 1=11 4+ 3+ 3+ 4+ 4+ 3=21
1+1=2 2+1=3 23, or 2+3=5

Translation: A stone fallen from heaven.

4—
L A P I S L A P S U S E X C A E L U S
4 1 3 3 5 4 1 3 5 2 5 5 4 3 1 5 4 2 5
(4+1=5)

3355 355 355

4+1+ 2+ 5+4+ 1+ 4+2=23

5— L A P I S E L I X I R

4 1 3 3 5 5 4 3 4 3 4

3355

4+1+ 4+3+4+3+4=23

The Grail Maiden Princess from 'Parcival'.

6— R E P A N S E D E S C H O Y E

4 5 3 1 1 5 5 4 5 5 3 2 2 5 5

355 355

(translates to the French motto)

7— R E P O N S E D E C H O I X

4 5 3 2 1 5 5 4 5 3 2 2 3 4

33555

(translates to the English motto)

8— C H O S E N R E S P O N S E

3 2 2 5 5 1 4 5 5 3 2 1 5 5

355 355

2+2+1=5 4+5+5+2+1=17

5+1+7=13

(translation of 'Royal Blood')

9— S A N G R A A L

5 1 1 1 4 1 1 4

3 3 5 + 5 (Order)

10— S A N G R E A L

5 1 1 1 4 5 1 4

3 5 5

11— H O L Y   B L O O D
2 2 4 5   2 4 2 2 4
=13   =14 = 1+4=5

12— R O Y A L   B L O O D
4 2 5 1 4   2 4 2 2 4
=14, 1+4=5

(Grail Castle)

13—
C A S T E L L U M   P U E L L A R U M
3 1 5 1 5 4 4 2 5   3 2 5 4 4 1 4 2 5
355   355
1+ 1+ 4+4+2+5=17   2+ 4+ 4+ 1+ 4+ 2=17

(names of Grail Princess Maidens from Grail romances)

14— F L O R I E   D E   L U N E L
5 4 2 4 3 5   4 5   4 2 1 5 4
355
4+2+4+   4+5+   4+2+1+5+4=35, 3+5=8

16— A M P F L I S E
1 5 3 5 4 3 5 5
33555

17— C L A R I S C H A N Z E
3 4 1 4 3 5 3 2 1 1 1 5
3355
3+4+1+4+   2+1+1+1=17

18— G A R S C H I L O Y E

1 1 4 5 3 2 3 4 2 5 5

33555

1+1+4+ 2+ 4+2=14, 1+4=5

19— S C H O Y S I A N E

5 3 2 2 5 5 3 1 1 5

33555

20— P E R F E C T I O N

3 5 4 5 5 3 1 3 2 1

33555

21— P A R A D I S E

3 1 4 1 4 3 5 5

22— L I F E

4 3 5 5=17

355

23— D E A T H

4 5 1 1 2=13

3 5 5

The Book of the Holy Grail

by Joseph of Arimathea

Original translation by Thomas Jefferson, 1787
Retranslated by Henry Mercer, 1853

Edited by J.R. Ploughman

Introduction

The purpose of this book is to introduce the seeker to the Quest for the Holy Grail. Scores of books have been written on the subject. Most are simply an interpretation of the historical and literary Grail, which leave the seeker more confused than when he began the Quest. These types of books only confuse and distort the allegory of the Grail which holds its intrinsic keys.

Other books weave a variety of historicity and literary points together with hermetic and Kabbalistic philosophy under the auspices of New-A thought and practice. These books, while beneficial in a practical sense, show little of what the Grail actually is other than in a historical and literary sense. This is usually overlaid with imagined relationships and correspondences to totally unrelated magics, practices and philosophies.

In order to understand the Grail completely, one needs to have several keys. The seeker must accept that the Grail is one thing and one thing only, and not merely a doctrine which is subject to the whimsy of the individual and changeable by interpretation from seeker to seeker. It is incredible and irresponsible how authors can tout such shallow nonsense while they speak of the greatest mystery of the world and the heavens.

Even to simply start the first step of the journey of the Quest, the seeker need realize the above and become separated from the glorification of one's ego as it relates to wisdom and knowledge.

The keys to the Quest are simple and basic: The aim of the Quest is to restore the Wasteland, not to gratify an internal spiritual need. To do this, one must undergo a set of physical, spiritual and royal degrees. The Grail is the secret essence between the first love in the universe, between God and His Goddess wife. The Grail is only carried by the Grail Maidens/ Princesses, who must meet strict standards of behaviour to become worthy.

There is a ritual which is sacred above all of the Grail priesthood and family, called The Marriage of the Elements. It is the ritual which makes it possible to discover the Grail Princesses who will be able to lift the Curse on the Grail Family and restore the Wasteland.

It is a war between good and evil, in which those on the side of good wish to preserve and protect the Grail for the salvation of mankind, and those who are evil wish to hide or destroy it.

The Grail can be proven and demonstrated by a set of mathematical equations which only apply to American English. The United States of America is the Chosen Land, and Her language is the Chosen Language.

The path of the Grail also demands that the seeker realizes that Jeshua ben Jusef (Jesus) was NOT crucified, but lived for mankind. Without this belief, the seeker can never Quest for the Grail in purity, which the Grail demands.

This is the theology of the Holy Grail in its lesser form, which was written down by Joseph of Arimathea in 54AD, called the Book of the Holy Grail or Merovingian Bible. It was given to Joseph by the Neutral Angels who brought the Grail to earth from the Celestial Realm (heaven). And any work which opposes this theological doctrine which includes two books, this being the lesser or first, is not Grail.

The Book of the Holy Grail is a sacred text which sets down the Grail doctrine, by right of authority. To the many, both initiates and non-initiates, it reads as a tragic love story in which the principal character has a curse put on him by his father. Here, the son must reincarnate many times until he meets the Grail Princess, who holds the spirit of Yse (Goddess) inside her. She must give him the Chosen Response and fall in love with him in order to remove the Grail Curse. Grail Princesses are special females who are called and chosen by the Goddess Yse. They bear specific traits and qualities which separate them from other females and identify them as Grail Princesses.

To the initiate, The Book of the Holy Grail reads as a ritual allegory, whose aim it is, to give the seeker its ancient doctrine and a set of archetypes and images, by which to understand the supernatural and natural worlds. Here the seeker will learn the connection of one to the other, and place him or herself in the allegory. This allows the seeker to become free of the illusionary mundane world and achieve Illumination.

Both initiates and non-initiates will see and experience an ancient doctrine which demands faith, belief, ethics and a morality which requires a pure heart as a fundamental key to the Quest. They will see the folly of the modern world and find a freedom from its repression and oppression. Here will be found the freedom to escape the restricting dogma of the modern world which is guided by Lucifer, Lilith and the Triple Headed Hecate.

The real answer to the riddle of the Holy Grail comes into focus only when the seeker becomes annointed to the Grail priesthood and undertakes the degrees of the Royal Quest and applies the Divine Mathematics to the Quest.

—Adam-Patriarch

Definitions

Here are the definitions which will help you understand the Book of the Holy Grail.

Pre-Existence—The time of the Gods before the creation of the Earth.

Celestial Realm—The place of the pre-existence where all the Gods and Goddesses were immortal, perfect and infinite.

Tellestial Realm—The realm where the Spirit goes when it leaves the physical body. Here, through the Blessings of the Dead is created the surroundings chosen by the deceased, before death, for them to live in during death.

Terrestial Realm—Earth, where we are mortal, finite and imperfect.

Chosen Land—That place where the G.A.O.T.U. directs the Chosen People to live and spread the Priesthood of the Holy Grail. The Third Chosen Land is America.

Chosen Peoples—The peoples and their descendents who settled America.

Chosen Language—American English as it was spoken since the 1770's. Which was said to be the language of the pre-existence. It is also the language spoken in the Languedoc at the time of the First Family. There are still areas where American English is spoken.

Royal Order- The 8th. to 13th. degree High Priesthood of the

Holy Grail.

Royal Hierarchy—The Highest 8th. to 13th. degree High Priest, Princess, High Priestess, Summoner and Handmaiden.

High Priesthood—The 8th. to 13th. degree High Priests, Princesses and High Priestesses.

Priesthood—The 3rd. degree Priests and Priestesses who are within the 5 Spiritual Degrees.

High Priest—A Templar Priest of the 8th. to 13th. degree.

High Priestess—She who has entered the Spiritual Degrees.

Princess—A perfect High Priestess who has attained the 5th. Spiritual Degree, and will reach the 13th. Royal Degree.

Divine Priesthood—The Priesthood of the Holy Grail.

First Divine Priesthood—the Melchezedek Priesthood which was given to Adam and handed down to Joseph of Arimathea.

Second Divine Priesthood- The Priesthood of Jeshua the Teacher who created the office of High Priestess. That a High Priest and High Priestess would rule with 11 disciples.

Third Divine Priesthood- The High Priesthood created by the 5 Royal Hierarchy, the First Family.

Gods— Divine male entities in the Celestial Realm.

Goddesses—Divine female entities in the Celestial Realm.

Sacred Father—God, the Father of All in the Celestial Realm. The Great Architect of the Universe.

Divine Mother—Goddess, the Mother of All in the Celestial Realm.

Yse—Wife and consort of the First God, who was alone and absolute. He split himself in two and created Yse. He retained his Active side, she was given his Passive side.

Erebus—The name of God as Order.

Eris—The name of Goddess as Chaos.

Lady of the Grail—Yse.

Sophia—Yse.

Precious Lady of the Grail—Yse.

Great Architect of the Universe—The title of the First God, after he created the Terrestrial Realm.

Marriage of the Elements—The foundation ritual of the Grail Priesthood, which holds the secret and mystery of the Holy Grail, and may reveal She who is the Sacred Princess and She will, by Her Chosen Response to the High Priest, remove the Curse on the Grail Family.

Dispensation—A Divine Talent bestowed upon one of the High Priesthood by the Patriarch.

Divine Dispensation—A Divine Talent bestowed upon the High Priesthood by the G.A.O.T.U. and Yse.

Dispensations of the Priesthood—Blessings, Sealings, Initiation, Consecration, Blessing of the Dead, Royal Marriage.

Blessings—Prayers said for healing, exorcism, banishing ill forces, purification etc.

Sealings—Ritual and Prayers done to bond people to people and people to animals, people to talents, trades, virtues etc.

Initiation—An Oath Binding Ritual to the Priesthood which shows trust and ethics.

Consecration—A Ritual which makes a High Priest, High Priestess and Princess. It is a Sacred bond with the G.A.O.T.U., Yse and the High Priesthood.

Blessing the Dead—A Sacred Ritual in which the High Priesthood creates within the Tellestial Realm, the place that the deceased would like to live in perfection with all of his closest family and friends, interests, ambitions, loves etc.

Priests of the Dead—The High Priests who prepare the body of the deceased for burial.

Royal Marriage—A Sacred Wedding between a High Priest and a High Priestess (who is also a Princess), both being between the 8th. and 13th. degree. This Marriage lasts for all time and eternity, and the couple will reunite in all their incarnations on the Terrestrial Realm.

Divine Mathematics—A system of high mathematics based upon the number 5. This system of mathematics can reveal that which is of the Holy Grail, when used with the Chosen Language. All which is of the Grail can be proven and demonstrated with Divine Mathematics.

Patriarchal Blessing—An honor bestowed upon those of the 8th. to 13th. degree which informs them of their Divine Dispensations and reveals to them their lineage. It is only bestowed by the Patriarch.

Physical Degrees—There are 3 Physical Degrees which teach the aspirant of the Priesthood the ways of attaining Illumination.

Spiritual Degrees—There are 5 Spiritual Degrees, being; Quester, Protector, Guardian, Seeker and Holder. They are attained by the Illumination the Initiate has attained and his/her ability to understand the Grail Riddles and apply the Divine Mathematics to their answers. The Spiritual Degrees are confirmed by the Royal High Priesthood.

Royal Degrees—They are 5 and are above the Spiritual Degrees.

Divine Plan—The plan of T.G.A.O.T.U. to recreate the Gods and the Goddesses of the Celestial Realm into mortal, finite and imperfect people in the Terrestrial Realm.

Royal Quest—The Quest for the Holy Grail.

Purpose of Life—The Royal Quest.

Time of Chaos—The time when men of weak spirit will reincarnate as women, and women of weak spirit will reincarnate as men, where sexual confusion will take place. This is also the time when the Luciferian Rebellion will create wars, strife, famine, disease, plagues of the blood, drought and floods.

Fullness of Times—The end times when the war between good and evil will come to a head, where men and women will become enemies.

Melchezedek—The son of T.G.A.O.T.U. and Yse who was also a Major God in the Celestial Realm, and who came to the Terrestrial Realm as a Neutral Angel.

Balance—Order and Chaos within each individual.

Neutral Angels—The custodians of the Holy Grail who inspire people who are pure of heart to seek the Holy Grail.

Soul—The God Spirit which is attached to all of your incarnations.

Spirit—The Illuminated mind Intelligence which governs any one life during an incarnation.

Order—That which is active, the giver. Logic.

Chaos—That which is passive, the receiver, Emotion.

Fire & Air—The Male Elements of Order.

Water, Salt & Earth—The Female Elements of Chaos.

Bloodline—Those who are related to the Grail Family through blood.

Lineage—Those who are related to the Grail Priesthood through a Priesthood line of succession.
(Note: Both Bloodline and Lineage may be mixed.)

Holy Grail—The Secret and Mystery which goes back in time to God splitting himself and creating Yse, His mate, and refers to her Response to His love.

Chosen Response—The gift of love returned to God by Yse when He created Her. This is the same Chosen Response which the Princess must give the Fisher King, if she is to break the curse on the Grail Family.

Death Prayers—An account written by those of the Grail to be read at their funeral, which creates their surroundings in the Tellestial Realm.

Books of the Merovingian Bible.

Book of Nysia—Regarding the time when people were once Gods and Goddesses and the understanding of reincarnation, the lives of the Gods and Goddesses in the Pre-existence, their types and sex, the 5 Celestial Races and their intrinsic Dispensations. ch. 1-32 verses, ch 2-23 verses, ch 3-8 verses, ch. 4-23 verses, ch.5-8 verses.

Book of Tasia—Regarding how the mortals should imitate the Gods, the Third Luciferian Rebellion, instructions for housing the Divine Priesthood within the First Family. ch. 1-17 verses, ch.2-23 verses, ch.3-8 verses, ch.4-8 verses.

Book of Arnia—Regarding reincarnation and its pitfalls, thereof such as the shifting of gender. 23 verses.

Book of Theosos—Regarding the Luciferian Rebellion. 5 verses.

Book of Erycina—Regarding the nature of Gods and Goddesses, Gods and Goddesses of the Celestial Realm, Neutral Angels. Book 1-5 verses, Book 2-5 verses, Book 3-8 verses.

Book of Reysa—Regarding the three manifestations of the Melchezedek Priesthood.
Book 1-13 verses, Book 2-5 verses, Book 3—8 verses, Book 4-5 verses.

Book of Joseph The Patriarch—Regarding the three manifestations of the High Priesthood, the Luciferian Rebellion, the murder attempt on Jeshua the Teacher, the Second Chosen Land, 5 principles of the Priesthood, the duties of the Priesthood, the degrees of the Priesthood, how the family should expand and grow, the Curse upon the Grail Family. Book 1-8 verses, Book 2-8 verses, Book 3-13 verses, Book 4-8 verses, Book 5-13 verses.

2nd Book of Joseph The Patriarch-Regarding the creation of the Sacred Rites of the Holy Grail, explanations of the positions of the Priesthood, Grail Princesses, dispensations and ordnances, 5 Spiritual Degrees. Book 1-23 verses, Book 2-8 verses, Book 3-13 verses, Book 4-8 verses, Book 5-13 verses plus the story of the Grail Curse.

Book of Amberis—Regarding details of the Grail Princesses, details of the Grail Families, the Bloodline and Lineage, duties of the husband and wife, children and family, rules of marriage, Royal Marriage, birthing of children, death rites. Book 1—8 verses, Book 2-23 verses, Book 3-23 verses, Book 4-13 verses, Book 5-5 verses, Book 6-8 verses, Book 7-5 verses, Book 8-5 Verses.

Book of Therac—Regarding signs and omens which will mark the Fullness of Times. 13 verses.

Book of Varena—Regarding the way of Yse, and the Royal Princesses of the Holy Grail. Book 1-8 verses, Book 2-5 verses, Book 3-5 verses, Book 4-5 verses, Book 5-5 verses.

2nd Book of Varena—Regarding the signs which will indicate that the Luciferian Rebellion will manifest its tools. Book 1-17 verses.

Book of Nysia

WHEREUPON the Angel Nysia came unto Joseph of Arimathea, High Priest of the Melchezedek Priesthood, and Patriarch of the Holy Grail, and did impart unto him the mysteries of all peoples, who were once Gods, and gave him understanding of their lives, which would be lived again and again.

1—BEFORE the beginnings of existence, in the realm before, all Souls were Gods and Goddesses. All were perfect, yet they had no Balance, by which to judge their perfection.

2—And they did lack the Balance of Order and Chaos in their lives, and were merely neutral, which is neither good nor evil.

3—Yet, in their perfection they knew by instinct, that they must have order and Chaos, to truly know perfection.

4—And they became stagnant and discontent, through their perfection, for they had no way of knowing their perfection, thus they became aware of their imperfection.

5—A great council of the Gods was called, that they would discuss the problem of how to attain Balance, and perfect their Godhood.

6—And each God and Goddess attended, each unto their own dominion, whether lesser, greater, major or minor, each according to their own dispensation.

7—And each spoke in turn whether lesser or greater, major or minor, and each spoke from his own dispensation, no more and no less.

8—And they were led and directed by He who was the Father of all Gods and Goddesses, His children.

9—And they spoke together as a family.

10—Led by the Father, as all families should be, and in this manner.

11—And after speaking and giving thought to how Balance of Order and Chaos might be attained, the Father announced that the imperfection of the Gods was that they were immortal, and their lives were all, too perfect, as was their existence and their contentment, and herein they had become stagnant and lazy.

12—And He decreed that they would become mortal.

13—And the decision of the conference was that they should be made mortal, and live and die and learn, and earn their perfection and Balance, and this would take many lifetimes, and that at the end they would return to Godhood.

14—Each God and Goddess would become mortal and live in a physical place, each with their own attributes and purpose.

15—And a physical world would be created for them to inhabit, and it would be their world, but with pitfalls and trials and ordeals. And this world, unlike their own world would be designed to be imperfect, in order to challenge them, that they would overcome this challenge.

16—Here, would they be removed, to Quest for perfection.

17—And the Father of His children, being the oldest and wisest of all Gods, being a good Father, saw fit to be fair to his children in this decision, and He told them all that they should be able to remember their home and world, when they started to reach perfection as mortals.

18—And in this realm of the Gods, Yse, Mother of the Gods, and wife to the Father of all Gods and Goddesses, held the mysteries of the Grail.

19—Unto the Father is Wisdom and Knowledge, and unto Yse is Mysteries and Secrets and the Holy Grail.

20—And Her Secrets and Mysteries would, by decree, be given as a gift to mankind. And there would be one gift, sent from the realm of the Gods, to the realm of mortals. And for this gift, they would Quest. And upon finding this gift, and understanding it, they would cease to live many lives, and return to Godhood, in their own realm in the Celestial Realm, and regain their Godhood.

21—And here they would create their own Universe and Kingdom and as a Father and Mother, reign over it.

22—And by Divine Dispensation, through the Priesthood, could they seal unto them all those peoples who would follow them, to come to their Kingdom after their lives had been lived.

23—And they would become Lesser Gods and Goddesses. And they would be the people they were upon earth, but their Spirit, in the life they lived would become perfected.

24—Yet their Soul, that is the God of all their lives would still continue to have other lives, which would be of the Soul, but also of themselves, according to that life which they lived.

25—And by this Divine Dispensation of Sealing, even the Self who is Sealed to one who has refound Godhood, will still be bound to his own Soul, who was once a God in the pre-existence.

26—And this will give Wisdom to the God Soul, which will give Wisdom to those lives it creates, and the more one is Sealed in many lives, the more one is able to discover the Secret of Yse.

27—There is the Father, and Yse the Mother, and they are the parents of all the Gods in the old realm of the pre-existence. And their children are all the Gods and Goddesses, both male and female in nature. And each God and Goddess is a Soul. And each Soul is a God or Goddess. And each Soul is Spiritual, yet possesses physical bodies, which live and die. And they must Quest after the Secret of Yse, which is the gift to mankind, allotted by the Father of all Gods and Goddesses.

28—And each physical body which has life, is also by that body and that life, a Spirit, which can be Sealed to another for Eternity. And they are of the Soul, but are not of the other lives which are created by the Soul, except through their Knowledge.

29—Yet they may be linked together in other lives where they have gathered any Wisdom which will help them find the riddle of Yse, and all that will lead them on the Quest. And here they may remember.

30—And they would Quest and Quest, for there would be a memory that they would have a purpose to Seek a Divine Secret.

31—And the gift of Yse, would be Divine and freely given, as the key to the Mysteries of the abilities of the Gods. And the gift would be in plain sight, and overlooked by all save for those whose memory would, upon discovering the Divine Gift, remember the pre-existence. And would, remember a time when mortals were Gods.

32—And they would then enter the Priesthood on earth, which holds the Divine Dispensations of the Gods and the Mysteries of the Gods and Godhood which are Divine to Yse.

❁❁❁❁❁❁❁❁

Chapter 2

1—When the Father of the Gods decreed that all were to be made mortal, and suffer without Godly powers and Wisdom, there was rebellion.

2—The first begotten son of the Father and Yse was wise and knew that the decision of the Father to become mortal and find Order and Chaos was good.

3—The second begotten son of the Father and Yse, rebelled and said that Perfection did not need Order and Chaos, and he did not want to suffer as a mortal, when he could remain a God.

4—And he gathered others who also did not want to become mortal. And they confronted the Father and the Mother and they voiced their disagreement.

5—The Father felt saddened because two of his favourite

sons would be at conflict. But he knew it was part of His Divine Plan, and that the plan was now given a power of its own.

6—And the first son was Michael, and the second was Lucifer.

7—And the Father sought solitude, that He could meditate upon this problem in a fair and just manner.

8—And soon He returned. And He said unto the Gods and Goddesses, those of you who will obey me, stand at my right side, and those who would obey did so. And He instructed those who would rebel to stand at His left side, and they did.

9—And he turned to them and said, I am the oldest and wisest of you all. And even I must learn the extent of my Godhood, that even as we became discontent with our Perfection, was the Divine Plan ever unfolding. And that we were to find Balance of Order and Chaos that we could truly know Perfection, this is our purpose. For as we became aware of it, we have started to know it, as many of you obey and many of you rebel. Here is our first taste of Order and Chaos. And I decree my love for all of you, despite your choices to rebel against my Wisdom. And as I love all of you equally, I have made my decision in love and fairness to both sides of thought.

10—I will create unto you a mortal world. And each of you will become mortal as was my original decision. And half of you will go in Order, and half in Chaos, as is determined by your choice. And upon becoming mortal, I will give you the freedom of Will and freedom of Choice to act in Order or Chaos.

11—And I will design your mortal world as this world, save it will not be perfect as you know it, but will have many obstacles. And it will be your duty to overcome these obstacles and become Perfect in the Wisdom and Knowledge of Order and Chaos.

12—And I shall send to your world, Neutral Angels which will bring the gift of Yse, your Mother, that which determines all creation and change, which I gave unto Her as a token of my love for Her.

13—And it will be a contest for each of you to locate this Divine Gift. And if those of Lucifer find it first, and keep it from your brothers and sisters, and hide it from them, you shall all be returned to Godhood, without ever knowing or learning Order and Chaos. But, be warned, you will suffer discontentment as will your brothers and sisters, and the plan will even yet at some other future time only have to be enacted again.

14—And if those who obey me, under my son Michael, find the Divine Gift through Wisdom and purity of heart, and they secure the Divine Priesthood, they shall have use of the Divine Secret of Yse, and will be granted my Dispensation to use it to overthrow the rebellion of Lucifer and his followers.

15—Those of you under Michael will go in goodness. Those who choose Lucifer, will go in evil, and here you all go in free Will and free Choice.

16—And you all shall live many lives in many times, and shall shift lives from one time to another according to your Path of Wisdom, that to you, as Souls, there will be no measurable time, but only place, that you shall shift forward and backward as you will.

17—And you shall be as you are now, in your many lives.. Gods will be men and Goddesses will be women. And changes from man to woman or woman to man, in other lives will be due to confusion in life, and no change will be permanent, nor will these changes be often if at all for many of you, and you will strive to become what you were, as you can only return to Godhood, Pure to how you started.

18—And you shall have many Gods and Goddesses to guide you. Those who are pure and good and without impurity, and in truth will be reflections of your Father and Mother.

19—And you will know us as we will be as we are now. I as the Father, being Active, and Yse as the Mother, being Passive.

And here seek Balance. And reject any God who is passive and any Goddess who is active, for they will be creations of Lucifer and his sister, designed to keep you from the Quest and the Divine Secret of your Mother, Yse.

20—The Divine Secret is to be found within and without Yse, and carried only by women which are of Her. And only they, will become High Priestesses and Princesses in the Divine Priesthood of my third and most wise son, Melchezedek.

21—And only a man will be able to release and direct the Divine Secret of Yse, and these men will be the High Priests, of the Priesthood entrusted to my wisest son Melchezedek.

22—As I gave Yse the Divine Secret as my gift of love to Her, and as Her gift of love with me, so she shares it with me. All High Priests shall have the duty to be of myself, the Father, granted to bring forth the Divine Secret and its power from the High Priestesses and Princesses who are as Yse, the Mother, and be as Her in their Divine Priesthood. And this Divine Secret will be well hidden, openly, yet only understood by him who is of me, and she who is of Yse. And it shall be called the Holy Grail, only to be bourne by Maidens, and only to be directed by Kings. And its secrets shall be hidden in the language of the Chosen Peoples and it shall be proven by Divine Mathematics in equations known only to the True and Only Priesthood. And though, in the beginning, the language and Divine Mathematics will not manifest, the Secret shall. And towards the end, when the Priesthood is built up, they will come together. And, even at times when few hold the Priesthood and the Secret be not revealed. One of you shall be reborn with this knowledge, and will preserve, protect and guard it above all else.

23—And with the wave of His hand, the Father created the Universe and all in it, to house the Divine Secret of His consort and wife, Yse, most Precious Lady of the Grail. And He became the Great Architect of the Universe, all Creator, all

Designer, all Mathematician, that through all He is, He could impart Himself to the world and peoples He created.

Chapter 3

WHEREUPON Nysia did impart unto Joseph of Arimathea, knowledge about how the lives of the Soul would live again and again, that he should understand all of these things and impart them to the High Priesthood in their teachings of the Wisdom of Mankind.

1—The physical world, being the realm of mortals is governed by time. That the beginning goes unto the end.

2—And all mortals live within this time, beginning at a time and living unto a time whereby their life will end. And that time of life is given unto that life that it may Quest for the Holy Grail.

3—And, that life is a Spirit unto itself, and is all that it has learned and experienced, and no more and no less.

4—And upon death, that Spirit returns to the Soul which was once a God in the pre-existence.

5—And the Spirit of that life will add its Wisdom and Knowledge to the Soul from which it came. This is the natural order of the Divine Plan of T.G.A.O.T.U.

6—Forthwith, another life will be created by the Soul. That it will be reborn in the mortal realm, and here take up the Quest where the life before left off. And this may be in the future of the life before, or in the past of the life before, or at the same time as the life before, that two Spirits in one life may exist from the same Soul.

7—And this will be enacted according to the next step of Knowledge, which will lead you closer to the Divine Secret, that each life will occur at a time which will best help your

Quest.

8—And in those lives which you are close to the Divine Secret, be it that you know it or not, you will remember other lifetimes through your link to the Soul, where all memory of those lifetimes are housed.

Chapter 4

WHEREUPON the Angel Nysia, did impart to Joseph of Arimathea how the Gods of the pre-existence lived and their types and sex.

1—In the realm of the Gods there were 5 races. And they were each of a particular Dispensation.

2—And unto each was their Dispensation special, and, to each other did they teach, that all the races of the Gods may learn from each other, their special and perfect Dispensations.

3—And if a God of one race became wiser, in the Dispensation of the Gods of another Dispensation, they also being another race, the God who became wiser in that Dispensation of the other race, than his own Dispensation, may, at will, change his race, and become of the Dispensation of which he developed much talent.

4—And within all races of the Gods there were lesser and greater, major and minor. And he who would change, would only be he, who within his own race was minor or lesser, and could aspire to be major or greater with his new found Wisdom.

5—And hereby, he would ask the G.A.O.T.U. who was the Father, for a Sealing to the new Wisdom and the other race. And it would be granted to him.

6—For the G.A.O.T.U. is the truest Father and loves his children each as the other, and revels in their attainment of wisdom and happiness and their pursuit of excellence of life, liberty to choose, and freedom of will, to be what they are, no less and no more.

7—Each race of the Gods was divided into male and female, that the Gods would have unto them as their right, all which was masculine and active in their Dispensations. And the Goddesses, would have unto them, as their right, all which was feminine and passive in their Dispensations.

8—And to each was the display and Wisdom of their Dispensations, being Active and Passive, as their sex decreed.

9—And here was contained both sides of the Dispensation. It was decreed by the Father, the oldest and wisest God, that to make the Dispensation complete, Gods and Goddesses must marry, and that marriage would be the Most Sacred Dispensation, that here the Dispensations of the God and Goddess would be complete.

10—Here would be a complete Dispensation, both Active and Passive, in Balance.

11—And each God and Goddess to be married, would be married only unto a God or Goddess of their race and Dispensation, that here they could Balance their Dispensations together, with their elements of Active and Passive.

12—For this would make their Dispensations whole and complete. And it was decreed by the Father, the G.A.O.T.U. that they should marry only unto their own race of God and Dispensation.

13—That to marry outside their race and Dispensation was to be to no avail, as the purpose of marriage was to complete and Balance both the Active side and the Passive side of the Dispensation.

14—And the Father, being fair and wise, decreed that, if a God or Goddess of one race or Dispensation, came to love a Goddess or god of another Dispensation, the God or Goddess who was lesser in the Dispensation of their race, would learn and attain greatness in the Dispensation of the race of who they chose for marriage. And they would become of that race, and make a union with a Balanced marriage.

15—A God may only marry a Goddess, and a Goddess may only marry a God, and this is Balance of Active and Passive of a Dispensation.

16—Passive may not marry with Passive, and Active may not marry with Active, nor God to God, nor Goddess to Goddess.

17—The G.A.O.T.U. and Yse, Sacred Lady of the Grail, are the Father and Mother of all Gods and Goddesses, who are their children. And they are known by many names, which have been discovered by those who Quest. And the most important of these are Erebus, God of Order, and Eris, Goddess of Chaos.

18—And the G.A.O.T.U. imparted the Holy Grail unto Yse, His consort and wife, as a token of His love for Her. And from this love, their children were begotten. And their children held within them, parts of the sacred union of He who is God, and She who is Goddess.

19—And the Gods held the Active Wisdom and the Goddesses held the Passive Wisdom. And each developed talents, which were to determine their Dispensations and purpose. And to be recognized they developed into races determined by their Dispensations. And no race was above the other. And together they all formed the parts of the Father and the Mother.

20—The Father, oldest and wisest of all Gods, who was First among them, was in the beginning, alone. In His loneliness, He made a division within himself and Spirit, in two, and He created Yse to be His mate, and to love. Here was the first part of the Divine Plan. Yet He was both Active and Passive in the beginning, and was Absolute, with His own creation, He would become only Active. The creation of Yse, was out of love, and unto Her, His Passive half given.

21—That He shall rule the Active Wisdom and She shall rule in the Passive Wisdom. And he held the Active keys of creation and She held the Passive keys of creation.

22—He the giver, She the receiver, together in Creation, and Balance, and completeness of Dispensation of all the Wisdoms.

23—And together they gave life to their children who were both Gods and Goddesses, after the manner of their parents. And the realm of the Gods was perfect and of Order and immortal and infinite. And they became discontent, and the decision was made for them to be removed from the realms of the Gods, and to be reborn in Chaos, imperfect and mortal and finite. That they would attain Balance so once more they could return to the Celestial realm of the Gods to be truly perfect.

Chapter 5

WHEREUPON the Angel Nysia spoke unto Joseph about the Celestial Races.

1—THERE were 5 Celestial Races of the Gods and Goddesses. Each to their own special and divine Dispensation. Some greater, some lesser, some major, some minor. Yet all were loved equally by the G.A.O.T.U. and Yse, His consort and wife and Mother to the Gods and Goddesses.

2—And, each one of the Celestial Races was recognized by color, that all should know the Wisdom of the others.. And all were perfect in their different beauties, and without flaw in both their physical beauty, or their spiritual Wisdom.

3—The Red Celestial Race held the Divine Dispensations of Spirituality and Religion.

4—The White Celestial Race held the Divine Dispensations of Language an Mathematics.

5—The Black Celestial Race held the Divine Dispensations of Wisdom and Architecture.

6—The Brown Celestial Race held the Divine Dispensations of Magick and Philosophy.

7—The Yellow Celestial Race held the Divine Dispensations of Healing and Divination.

8—And they lived in harmony, each willing to teach and be taught by the other, that they should have a better understanding of the other Dispensations.

Book of Tasia

THE angel Tasia visited unto Joseph of Arimathea, Highest of the High Priests of the Divine Priesthood sent to mankind by T.G.A.O.T.U. to protect the secrets of Yse, Divine Lady of the Holy Grail. And she spoke unto Joseph of how mankind would be and the understanding thereof, and how mankind should imitate the Gods of their Souls.

1—ALL of mankind was created from their former selves which were the Gods and Goddesses of the Celestial Realm.

2—And here in imitation they would be created in the Terrestrial Realm by the G.A.O.T.U. And they would be created as they were in the Celestial Realm, yet in a state of being mortal, imperfect and finite.

3—And they would remain, by their Souls how they were as Gods and Goddesses when they were immortal, perfect and infinite, in both their Celestial Race and their sex.

4—And they would once again return to Godhood within their own Celestial Race and sex.

5—And in the Terrestrial Realm they would have many lives, in many times, and they would Quest after the Divine Secret of Yse, given to Her by Her Divine Husband the G.A.O,T.U.

6—And this Divine Secret would be the Divine Key to Order and Chaos, and Creation called the Holy Grail. And it would only be found in She who is Divine to Yse, Goddess of Goddesses.

7—And within He who would find the Divine Secret called the Holy Grail, would be the Key to manifest the Grail in She who housed it. And this is what is meant by a God being Active and a Goddess being Passive. That only She holds the power, and only He can manifest it from Her.

8—And they who were pure of heart would accept the Gift of the Quest, as it is the Gift from He who is God and She who is Goddess, which will allow you to reach Perfection and your Godhood once more.

9—And, there is 5 parts to the Royal Quest. And only those who are pure of heart and true to themselves may enter the contest of the Quest, as they know the Purpose of Life.

10—There be 5 parts to the Royal Quest, for 5 is a sacred number. And the 5 parts of the Royal Quest each has its place, and each part makes up the whole. And each part is a Spiritual Degree which gives the Questor Illumination. And each part when discovered never leaves the Soul of the Questor, even if he is reborn again at another time and another place will he remember the Spiritual Degree he has earned, for he will be Pure of Heart.

11—The First Spiritual Degree is the Questor. Here is the Quest for the Truth, Knowledge and Wisdom which is to be discovered in the Holy Grail. Here the Key is Belief.

12—The Second Spiritual Degree is the Protector, who is willing to Protect the Holy Grail, though they know not what it is. Here, the Key is Faith.

13—The Third Spiritual Degree is Guardian. Here the man or woman on the Royal Quest vows to Guard all things which concern the Holy Grail. Here they may start to learn what the Grail is, and recognize its power and what it can accomplish. Here the key is Devotion.

14—The Fourth Spiritual Degree is the Seeker. Those who have earned this Degree have discovered what the Grail is, and pledge to seek it, that it may be used in times of trouble. The Key to this Degree is Illumination.

15—The Fifth Spiritual Degree is Holder. Here the Divine Secret is revealed. For the men of the Holy Grail go Secretly into the world on the Quest to locate the Grail, that it may be used in times of need and trouble, for peace, harmony and the service of any peoples in need. The men of the Grail have the province of directing the Divine Dispensations and Powers of the Holy Grail.

16—Women who become Holders of the Holy Grail, and attain the Fifth Spiritual Degree, go into the world Openly with the Grail to do their service for mankind.

17—And they shall seek each other out, who are of the Fifth Spiritual Degree, and they shall marry and create a Grail Bloodline, that there shall be a Royal and Divine Family Lineage in which the children of the father and mother will be instructed in the ways of the Holy Grail, and the Divine Priesthood, given by God to His wisest son Melchezedek, to bring to the people of the Terrestrial Realm, to guard the Grail and use its Divine Dispensations wisely.

Chapter 2

HERE Tasia informed Joseph that the Third Luciferian Rebellion was upon the Terrestrial Realm, and it was time to house the Divine Priesthood in his family for safe keeping.

1—Joseph, I give unto you, warning. The Third Luciferian Rebellion is upon all of us. You must protect the High Priesthood. You must leave this land with your family, for it is cursed and no longer pure.

2—You have done well as a trader and merchant, and you can provide ships and have many allies in far places. Gather up your family and leave. For the Luciferian Rebellion has cast a hatred on the land and will execute your son Jeshua the Teacher.

3—But you shall tell no one of your plan, for it might fall upon evil ears.

4—Soon, the Luciferian Rebellion will have your son arrested, even to forcing the Sanhedrim to go outside their own sacred laws, and even here the enemies of the G.A.O.T.U. have power. He is your son, and after you, the last Holder of the Divine Secrets of the Holy Grail, and neither you, nor any of the other High Priests is young enough to father sons to take your place.

5—The Luciferian Rebellion will have won if they murder your son, Jeshua the Teacher. And should they succeed, they will capture the Holy Grail and hide its Divine Secret from mankind and all will perish. They will carry it back to the Celestial Realm and there overthrow the G.A.O.T.U. and rule the Terrestrial Realm in evil and Chaos, that even mankind shall become as discontent in their imperfect existence as the Gods once were in their Perfect existence. But, from here there shall be no escape, as the Grail will be gone from them perhaps forever, and Yse will die.

6—Know that the G.A.O.T.U. has great powers, but even those who follow His evil son are of Him and have Wisdom. Know also that when He created this Terrestrial Realm, your world, did He foresee that this could occur.

7—And know that with this foresight the G.A.O. T.U. knew that you were the last High Priest who could father a son, and that His Spirit entered you when you impregnated your wife Mary, she herself a High Priestess of the Holy Grail, and a Holder of the Divine Secret, and your son Jeshua the Teacher, was also the good son of the G.A.O.T.U. who was Michael in the Celestial Realm of the pre-existence.

8—Know that he is Divine, and from his blood, and that of Grail women who hold the Fifth Spiritual Degree can come a Divine and Sacred Bloodline and Lineage, wherein the Divine Secret

and Essence of the Holy Grail will forever dwell. And if you can save the life of thc son with two Fathers, one physical and one spiritual, the blood of Jeshua the Teacher will be preserved and he will save his Spiritual Mother, Yse, Divine Goddess of the Holy Grail, and she will not die.

9—Go unto your son Jeshua the Teacher, and tell him this, and he will know it. Tell him to inform the Lesser Priesthood that he leads, that he must leave them, and for them to scatter and go into the land and Seek all those of the Female Race who Hold the Grail by Instinct and Nature.

10—Tell not your wife nor your son's High Priestesses, and prepare your escape. There are also those soldiers who can be bribed, who will help you save your son.

11—It is the intent of the Rebellion to claim your son after they have murdered him, for their own, thereby capturing and imprisoning his Divine Spirit. They will make it appear that he had to die for mankind to save them, and they will build their Rebellion around Him, and mankind will suffer and the G.A.O.T.U. will have no power to stop it.

12—Jeshua the teacher must live for mankind, that one day his bloodline may vanquish over the Luciferian Rebellion.

13—And, know this, even the lesser Priesthood believes he is dead, there are those amongst them who will lose heart. And even that he lives, secretly, the Luciferians will win the battle. And they will create religions which glorify their false victory, and these religions will become the enemy of the peoples of the Holy Grail, and the true Priesthood. And they will kill and murder any who try and preserve the High Priesthood and its Divine Mystery. And they will strike fear into peoples hearts. And they will repress their freedom of choice and will, Divinely given freely as a gift from T.G.A.O.T.U. to all His children as mortals.

14—And they will destroy all which is not as they are, all in the name of the Divine Son, and to them murder and torture will be justified as good. And the simple pleasures of mankind, and the right to question and learn will be judged evil and corrupt. And fear will reign for 2000 years upon the Terrestrial Realm.

15—And the Luciferian Rebellion will become the religion of the world, even to destroying other religions who exist in faith and true belief. And they will hold the power of monarchs in their hands and rule through them, and destroy through them.

16—And they shall seek to destroy the Divine Essence of the Grail which is the right of the women who chooses to be of Yse, and they will repress all women against the joys of love and union with men, lest they should meet a man of the Grail who will Balance the Grail, within her, and make her aware of her Grail Essence.

17—And this, the false prophets and false religions will they do to deprive mankind of the Royal Quest and the High Priestesses and Princesses. That here, will they hurt the High Priesthood of the Holy Grail. And here will they hurt Yse by robbing Her of Her Divine Essence.

18—And in the end of time, mankind will grow both wise to the ploys of the false religions and false prophets who are bathed in hypocrisy and sour to Truth. For here, the Luciferian Rebellion will tire, yet here they will have poisoned mankind. And few will enter the True Priesthood of the Prophet and High Priest, Melchezedek. And there will be a time of great Chaos as the aftermath of the Rebellion.

19—Yet the Luciferian Rebellion will only be resting, at this time, being the time of Chaos, there shall be many signs. And this time shall mark the turning point of the Luciferian Rebellion, and here, those of the Holy Grail must vanquish, over our enemy.

20—In this time of Chaos, the essence of the Luciferian Rebellion will have infected all of mankind. And from its poison, peoples will have drunk. And many will join on the side of evil, though they know it not.

21—And the female race will turn on itself from the poison

it has drunk from the false prophets and false religions who deprived them of Yse and Her Divine Essence. And they will try and seek her, but will not do so in purity of heart, but in bitterness and ignorance. And they will only find a reflection of that bitterness and ignorance. And here they will create their own false prophets and false religion, believing it to be true, but finding it empty and void of Yse. For here, they will only find the evil of the Triple Headed Hecate, who bellows fire and smoke. By her fire and smoke will they adopt her evil ways, and fire and smoke will be their sign, for they will have forsaken Yse and the Sacred Living Water of the Holy Grail.

22—And hereby, shall they deprive themselves and each other of their race, from their right to Yse, Divine Goddess of the Holy Grail. And they shall deprive themselves of freedom of choice and will, and they shall do so in bitterness, which they will direct in ignorance. And they shall hate all of their race who try to embrace Yse, without bitterness and in understanding. And they who follow are led by the Triple Headed Hecate, shall be jealous and angry that their are those of the female race who will not share in their hatred and bitterness.

23—And in this time of Chaos, the weakest willed men will become as women and the weakest willed women will become as men, and they shall hate one another, and have much bitterness towards one another. Here they shall have fallen away from T.G.A.O.T.U. and Yse, Divine Goddess, Lady of the Grail. And in this time, the hardest time of life in the Terrestrial Realm, when they most need the Royal Quest, and the Holy Grail, most will have fallen and turned to the Luciferian Rebellion for hope.

Chapter 3

1—THIS will not be a time of promise or truth. It shall be a time of madness and strife, of famine and death, of slander and false witness, of floods and of drought, of much hate and confusion.

2—It will be a time of giving up and surrender.

3—It will be a time when personal glory will reign over truth, and mankind will resign itself to defeat. And wives will turn on their husbands, and they on their lives, and this shall so the children also do. And slander and false witness will destroy the family, and likewise the harmony of husband and wife.

Willed in the Terrestrial Realm.

4—And Lucifer and his kind will rejoice. For now, his side will outnumber the side of Michael. And while many will feel that they oppose him, their actions will show that they serve him. And he will take from them, their joy and happiness, truth and beauty, gentleness and love, and leave them to the emptiness of the Triple Headed Hecate.

5—And they shall have dominion over many, and make their thoughts and blood run cold with bitterness and hate.

6—Yet, in the Balance of Proportions, those who follow the Grail. and protect it will have greater power in it, than if they had numbers equal to those of Lucifer and Hecate.

7—And for their small number, those of the Holy Grail will have great strength and conviction.

8—And they will not cease to help mankind, nor be blinded by hate and bitterness. For even they know how to defeat Lucifer, who was called by the name Adamas in the pre-existence, he who is the Lion Faced, whose dominion is over the Self Willed in the Terrestrial Realm.

Chapter 4

1—THE Time of Chaos shall be a time of great obstacle, trial and ordeal for the High Pricsthood. In this time, the Grail Family will have split many times, and most will not know of the others, and some will not know of the High Priesthood.

2—But there shall be those who reject the ways of the Time of Chaos. And they will sense that they belong to something, but know not what.

3—And their instincts will tell them that they remember a time of the Father and Mother, and they shall seek religions which lay claim to have these as a God and Goddess. And they will remember something familiar about all of this, yet they will grow displeased of how the doctrine explains the Mysteries.

4—And here they shall only find a desperate attempt at instinct and slight remembrance, and a grasping at a shadow.

5—And yet, here is hope, for in the display of seeking to find the Supreme God and Goddess, Yse, coupled and not singly, is the instinct and slight remembrance promised us by the G.A.O.T.U. That when we were created mortal, we remember the words of our Father, who said unto us that He and Yse would always be with us, but there would be those Gods and Goddesses of the Luciferian Rebellion which would thwart us from our Purpose of Life.

6—And there will come she, who will rise above bitterness and hate, and self entrapment. And she will embrace Yse, and be as Her. And she will find that which she seeks, and it will Purify her. And she will have come back to the family, and know it well. And she will have within her the Holy Grail, and become of the Fifth Spiritual Degree.

7—And she will tell others who have the spark of remembrance in them, but who are misguided and deluded by false ways, to Perfection through Knowledge of a God and Goddess who impart the Mysteries. And she shall make clear to them her path. And they shall question it, and understand it and make it their own.

8—And this shall be the time the Fisher King will be allowed to die.

Book of Arnia

IN which the Angel Arnia appeared unto Joseph and spoke to him of the many facets in the incarnation of lives which would befall people. And she gave understanding to these things, so people would understand those, whose incarnations shifted from their original Celestial Race and sex. And this she did, so those who found this hindrance to be upon them would know why it was so and how it did occur.

1—All of the Gods and Goddesses in the Celestial Realm were begotten from the Sacred Father and Divine Mother, and all were born immortal as a God or as a Goddess, some lesser, some greater, some major and some minor. Each according to their Dispensation and Purpose.

2—And the Sacred Father, the first, oldest and wisest of the Gods, made each of His children mortal, and created for them a mortal world where they could learn Perfection from imperfection. And they could learn the secret of Balance, being Order and Chaos. And when He created the Universe, He Himself became The Great Architect of the Universe.

3—And in this physical world, called the Terrestrial Realm, the Gods would incarnate as males, and the Goddesses as females, both mortal and imperfect.

4—And they would also have many incarnations in the mortal world, in order to Quest for the Gift of Yse, which was the Chosen Response of Yse, to His Gift of Love to Her. And it is called the Holy Grail.

5—And each man would incarnate to again become a man, as would women incarnate to become women.

6—And the sign of the Fourth Luciferian Rebellion, would be that a man might incarnate as a woman. And here she would find attraction to a woman, as her instinct was, as a man in her incarnation before.And this may also happen to a woman incarnating as a man, and he would have the instinct to seek out a man to love.

7—And this will cause much confusion in both the life of the man and woman, and to those who have not had this experience.

8—It will cause strife for the man and woman who have this unfortunate experience, and find confusion in their Inner Nature. And many of these unfortunate people will rise up against those whose incarnations have stayed pure to the Natural Design of male and female. And they will have fallen prey to the Luciferian Rebellion, and by their confusion will have become part of it. For they will favour the fruit of their own loins, above understanding and Nature.

9—And those who accept this nature, and do not rise up against against the Natural design of man and woman, and who do not hate them, will not be influenced by the Luciferian Rebellion, as followers and slaves to its evil intention.

10—And the hunger of the loins above all else is a temptation which the Luciferian Rebellion will use against mankind to keep it from wisdom and knowledge.

11—Yet the hunger of the loins in love and honest pleasure is good. And here, it does not come before wisdom, knowledge and the Quest.

12—Let no strife or bitterness take you from the Quest, which is your rightful pursuit and purpose, and let no deceitful pleasures cloud your mind.

13—And let not a change in incarnation make you bitter and spiteful, but accept your life for it will change back to its Natural State in your next incarnation and all will be Balanced again.

14—And where there is a change in incarnation, and a man becomes a woman, for the first time, she will seek out both men and women. If he is to incarnate again as a woman, she will only seek out women. If the incarnation occurs out of Balance a third time she will seek out both men and women. A fourth time she will seek only women. A fifth time, the false she, will incarnate to Natural Balance as a man and seek out only women. This also does apply to a woman who incarnates to be a man.

15—And those who have had this change of incarnation, and who seek out their own sex are twofold. The first are they who are positive. And they are those who can accept and find contentment within and have no hate, anger or opposition towards those who are still within the Natural Design of mankind. And they are still with Michael.

16—Those who have this experience and who seek out others of the same sex, and hate those of the Natural Design, and try and usurp and overthrow those of the Natural design and hate their ways, are negative. And they will rebel against those of the natural design by creating false religions and harsh politics and evil power. They, are of the Luciferian Rebellion.

17—Yet, only the life which they are living will be dedicated to the Luciferian rebellion, for they will change back to their Natural State. And if they learn by chance, the True Balance, they may in their life escape the Luciferian Rebellion.

18—For we have the choice of Good or Evil, to follow Michael or to follow Lucifer, or to Quest or not to Quest.

19—Yet be not deterred, for we have no choice at birth, what path we follow. For it is determined by experience and how we perceive our Selves and lives. And though there be two paths to walk, with careful Wisdom and much thought, the path may be changed. And know well that those who accept the Royal Quest, will take up the Quest, and have a choice at birth to take up where they left off, in the life before.

20—The side of Michael demands facing Truth and putting aside your lesser passions and negative thoughts, in favor of Truth. Here you follow the Quest of the Grail according to your

Spiritual Degree. And simply to Believe in the Quest makes you Pure, regardless of your Spiritual Degree.

21—The side of Lucifer is the easily travelled path, whereupon you speak false wisdom and become Self Willed, and change Truth to suit your bitter life's experiences. Here you merely have to avoid learning, and simply create false explanations and reject those things which would take discipline to learn, and to laugh in the face of truth.

22—The Neutral Angels will strive to teach and guide you, to keep you from folly. Know them when they come to you, for they will be like people, only with a calmness. They are the last of the Grail Race from the Celestial Realm, and know, and live by the the writings of the Grail, yea all of the writings, without deterring from one word.

23—Know that in the True Nature of the Holy and Royal Quest, only a Watery and Passive female can hold the Holy Grail and be a Grail Maiden. And only a Fiery and Active male can give life to the Grail within her and bring it forth. And here, is True Purity in Balance betwixt Male and Female.

Book of Theosos

Whereupon the Luciferian Rebellion is explained.

1—THE First Luciferian Rebellion occurred during the time of the Celestial Realm, when Lucifer, brother of Michael, sons of the Great Father.

2—The Second Luciferian Rebellion was when two great forces were at conflict during the time of the Seeking of Knowledge in the Terrestrial Realm and Enoch erected the Temple of the Nine Arches, and all was destroyed in the Great Flood.

3—The Third Luciferian Rebellion took place when the Luciferian Rebellion tried to kill your son, Jeshua the Teacher. And you escaped to France with your son Jeshua, your wife Mary and the two High Priestesses of the Grail, Mary of Bethany and Mary of Magdala, who were unto your son, a High Priest of the Melchezedek Priesthood.

4—And here became the Fourth Luciferian Rebellion when they made him a martyr and created a false religion which will rule for 2000 years by fear and superstition and whose truth will be murder and torture and repression, and they will take the lands of the peoples and be hypocrites in their own cause. And in the end times of this Rebellion when they have all but won and suppressed the Grail, the signs will be wars, strife, famine, floods, drought, devestating disease and plagues, false witness and slander and weak men will act as women, and weak women will act as men. And there will be Chaos in the lands, and false prophets will reign. And they will deprive females of the Holy Grail, by making them fiery. And women will take smoke and fire into their lungs, and bellow fire. Know well that here, the Triple Faced Hecate will have gained dominion over females. And, together with Lilith, the Hairy Fiend of the Night, they will deprive all females from the beauty and gentle nature of Yse.

5—The time of the Fifth Luciferian Rebellion is twofold, and being the Fifth Period of the Terrestrial Realm, will be a time where Order or Chaos may rule. This is dependant upon the Fourth Luciferian Rebellion. If Order rules, the Grail will be restored upon the Terrestrial Realm and mankind can live in freedom and harmony, each race among the other, and all people with all animals, with the Divine Earth. No wars or famine & etc. will trouble us, and peace will be with us. Yea, if those of the Luciferian Rebellion capture and hide the Grail from mankind there will be a time of hatred among the 5 Celestial Races and warmongering and strife among men and women. And there will be a false peace which shall be ruled by evil rulers who look upon all peoples as slaves. And people will lose their way and accept their fate.

Book of Erycina

Book One

WHEREUPON the Angel Erycina told Joseph of Arimathea of the Nature of Gods and Goddesses, that he could impart this Wisdom to the peoples, that they would have understanding.

1—KNOW that the Sacred Father, the G.A.O.T.U. and Yse, the Divine Mother, Lady of the Grail are the First Parents. And that they Watch over us always.

2—To all peoples of all lands they manifest unto those peoples according to their needs and their ways of life. To be worshiped and honored.

3—And know in truth, that if they be true, the Father creates the power from the Mother, that She holds the power, but can not manifest it alone, and He only can manifest it from Her.

4—And he is Fire and Air, and She is Water, Earth and Salt.

5—Yea, the Luciferian Rebellion will create false Gods and Goddesses. And here know them for they will demand sacrifice, and will not be timeless. And they will demand hatred and bitterness. And their fathers will be weak and strengthless and the mothers will not be gentle and loving, and will be dominant and have hate before the father. And they must be shunned.

Book Two

WHEREUPON the Angel Erycina imparted the Wisdom of understanding of the Gods and Goddesses of the Celestial Realm.

1—FIRST and oldest of the Gods was the Great Father, who dwelled alone absolute in the great void before the Universe was created. And he was lonely alone. But being absolute, he was both Order and Chaos, being logic and emotion. And he created for himself a wife, made from his own being. And she was given the name Yse, and was pure and perfect and became his Balance as he hers. And he gave her the gift of love, which was the first love, given freely. And when she received this love, her emotion spilled freely from her, as a sign of her receiving his love. And this became the chosen response of love and as the first love, the true sign of love. And from Yse, the Holy Grail was born.

2—And their first children, both Gods and Goddesses were the Major and oldest children, and they were first in the Sacred and Divine Dispensations of the Father and the Mother. And each mother taught their daughters the Chosen Response, and each father taught his sons to seek the Chosen Response in his chosen loves, and unto them to cleave.

3—And their begotten children were the minor Gods and Goddesses who shared the Divine Dispensations of their parents, and the wisdom of the Chosen Response.

4—And the begotten children of the Minor Gods and Goddesses held divers Divine Dispensations and shared the mysteries of the Chosen Response. And they were the Greater Gods and Goddesses.

5—And the begotten children of the Greater Gods and Goddesses were the Lesser Gods and Goddesses, who were to hold exact Divine Dispensations.

Book Three

IN which the Angel Erycina explained the Neutral Angels.

1—It is wrong to think that the Neutral Angels did not take sides. For they did, and chose the side of the Grail and Michael.

2—And we offered our service to remain as spirits, and not live as others, and this was our sacrifice, thus we are Neutral.

3—And we are both male and female, the males being of fire and active, and the females being of water and passive.

4—And those female Neutral Angels are many. And we come to those who are pure of heart and true in their Quest in both the spirit, with thoughts of guidance to help in the Quest, and we also appear in the physical, alive and mortal, to instruct and become Princesses of the Holy Grail, and inspire mortal females to win and hold he Grail.

5—And those who are males, inspire all females who give the Chosen Response to win and hold the Holy Grail.

6—We are of the first line of the children of the Great Father and Sacred Mother, being the Major Gods and Goddesses.

7—And some of us know our purpose and live it, and others do not, but carry the Dispensation of the Holy Grail.

8—And all whom we touch are made Sacred, if only for a while, yet they will always remember the effect we had upon them, especially the females who give the Chosen Response.

❀❀❀❀❀❀❀❀

Book of Reysa

Book One

Whereupon the Angel Reysa spoke unto Joseph of Arimathea about the three manifestations of the Melchezedek Priesthood.

1—MELCHEZEDEK was a Major God and the third son of the Sacred Father and Divine Mother. And when the Sacred Father became T.G.A.O.T.U. and created the Universe, he appointed Melchezedek as first among High Priests and the Divine Priesthood to guard and protect the Holy Grail.

2—And the Neutral Angels brought the Holy Grail to the Terrestrial Realm, that it may be the purpose of life in Quest, and this being the gift of the First Father and Mother to mortal man.

3—And the lineage and tribe of Melchezedek *(the 13th tribe also known as the Tribe of Arcadia, the lost tribe)* are to be the overseers and High Priesthood.

4—The G.A.O.T.U. imparted the mystery of the Grail to Adam, as first protector under the Melchezedek Priesthood.

5—Seth, son of Adam was the protector successor to the High Priesthood.

6—Seth passed the mystery to Enoch, son of Jared who was the sixth son in descent, of Adam. To him, T.G.A.O.T.U. appeared in a vision.

7—In the distance arose a mountain unto the heavens and Enoch was removed to the top thereof. There he beheld a magnificent triangular plate of gold, where within the center was engraved, an eye. Also engraved thereupon were strange characters of which he was strictly warned never to pronounce.

8—Presently he seemed to be lowered into the bowels of the

earth, through Nine Arches. Within the Ninth, or the deepest of which, he saw the same brilliant plate which was shown to him on the mountain.

9—Enoch, being inspired by the Most High, and in commemoration of this wonderful vision, built a Temple under ground. This happened in that part of the world which was afterwards called the land of Canaan, and since known as the Holy Land.

10—Enoch, in imitation of what he had seen, caused a triangular plate of gold to made, each side of which was a cubit long. In its center he engraved the Eye of the G.A.O.T.U., and around it he engraved the same ineffable characters which the G.A.O.T.U. had shown him. And he placed it on a triangular pedestal of white marble, which he deposited in the Ninth Arch.

11—When Enoch's Temple was completed, he received the following command, which was to make a door of stone, and let there be a ring of iron therein, by which it may be occasionally raised, and let it be placed over the opening arch, that the sacred matter enclosed therein may be preserved from the universal destruction now impending. And he did so, and none but Enoch knew of this precious treasure.

12—And behold, the wickedness of mankind increased more as they had not the full Knowledge of the Royal Quest. And a great Flood ensued, inspired by the Luciferian Rebellion, and the G.A.O.T.U. feared that He may have to destroy His creation and return to the Celestial Realm to start over again. But, Yse advised Him to use His Wisdom and to not destroy His Creation. For, in purity of heart, Enoch perceived that the Knowledge and Wisdom of the Gift was likely to be lost in the general destruction. And being desirous to preserve the principles of these sciences, for the posterity of those whom the G.A.O.T.U. would spare. He built two great pillars atop the highest mountain. He built one of brass, to withstand water and the other of marble, to withstand fire. And he engraved upon the marble pillar, characters signifying that there was a most precious treasure concealed in the Arches underground, which he had dedicated to the G.A.O.T.U. And upon the pillar of brass, he engraved the principles of the Divine Mathematics of the G.A.O.T.U.

13—The great flood took place and destroyed most of the great monuments of antiquity. The marble pillar fell in the general destruction, but by Divine Permission the pillar of brass withstood the water, by which the ancient state of Divine Mathematics has been handed down to us.

Book Two

1—AND the Priesthood passed onto Moses to whom God, T.G.A.O.T.U. did communicate His Divine Law. Moses was also given the true pronunciation of His Sacred Name, which He told to him, should be found by some of his descendants engraved upon a plate of gold.

2—Then the Priesthood was passed to Solomon, the wisest of the Kings. And he remembered the words of T.G.A.O.T.U. to Moses, that some of his descendants would discover His Sacred Name. And he knew by his wisdom that this could not be accomplished until he had erected and consecrated a Temple to T.G.A.O.T.U. in which he would deposit the precious treasures of the pre-existance.

3—He chose the most healthy and beautiful spot in Jerusalem for this temple. And upon digging for a foundation, they discovered the ruins of an ancient edifice, amongst which they found a very considerable quantity of treasure.

4—All the treasures were collected and carried to Solomon, who upon deliberation, concluded them to be the ruins of some ancient temple, erected before the flood, and possibly unto the service of idolotry. He then declined to build upon that spot, and chose another place, where the temple was erected.

5—And the temple of Solomon was built, to house, protect and guard the secrets and mysteries of the Holy Grail.

Book Three

1—AND Melchezedek, Highest of High Priests incarnated unto the Terrestrial Realm, and took his place by inheritance, in the line of succession. And he formed the First Priesthood, which before was a Guardianship.

2—The Priesthood from Adam to Solomon had the duty to Guard the Great Secret, and could communicate with the G.A.O.T.U.

3—But they knew not what they guarded, but they were devoted and had much faith.

4—And it was their duty to seek out and find and know certain types of males and females, and to arrange their marriages to begin the Sacred Bloodline upon the Terrestrial Realm.

5—And they taught about the Celestial Realm. And they Blessed the Dead, that they would incarnate without influence from the Luciferian rebellion. And they performed the Royal Marriage and Sealed the husband and wife together, that they would never be parted. And to each other, the High priesthood sealed themselves, so they would incarnate and come together again to Guard and Protect the Secrets of the Holy Grail.

6—And, upon Melchezedek being incarnated, he took up the High Priesthood and imparted unto it the 5 Spiritual Degrees above the 3 Physical Degrees. And he taught to the Priesthood the first rituals of allegory which would explain the Luciferian Rebellion, the Celestial Realm and the Divine Secret which is the Holy Grail.

7—And the Priesthood was passed to Joseph of Arimathea.

8—And Joseph passed the Priesthood on to his son, Jeshua the Teacher.

Book Four

1—AND forthwith, Melchezedek returned to his station as a Neutral Angel, and know now that Joseph of Arimathea will succeed him as Patriarch and Elder of the High Priesthood, as the Highest High Priest.

2—And Melchezedek was the wisest son of the G.A.O.T.U. and His Divine Consort Yse, and to the Terrestrial Realm did he bridge the Celestial Realm.

3—And this was the Priesthood upon the Earth.

4—And now the Priesthood must be confined to the Terrestrial Realm, for all mankind.

5—For here, the battle rages betwixt Order and Chaos. So be it that ye are chosen to be the Patriarch of the Holy and Divine Bloodline whose peoples will carry, care for, protect and guard the Holy Grail.

Book Five

1—THE first Priesthood was established from the Lineage of Adam to Joseph of Arimathea, and it was the Melchezedek Priesthood and its first part was as Guardians and Protectors of the Divine Dispensations of the Royal Secret of Yse.

2—And from this Guardianship, did Melchezedek create a Priesthood with 3 Physical degrees and 5 Spiritual degrees. And here, many were made High Priests.

3—The second manifestation of the Priesthood was with

Jeshua the Teacher, who, through Yse created the office of High Priestess.

4—The third manifestation of the Priesthood, would remove it from the First Holy Land to the Second Holy Land. And here it would become the Priesthood of the Holy Grail, within the Royal Bloodline. And here Joseph of Arimathea created the office of Princess.

5—And even again, the Priesthood would change, and it would do so for two more changes, that the Fifth would be perfect. And this shall not be until the Royal Priesthood reaches the Third Holy Land where there will dwell the Chosen Peoples. And they shall speak the Chosen Language, marked by the Divine Mathematics of the Holy Grail, which shall prove the Grail.

Book of Joseph the Patriarch

Book One

Whereupon I, Joseph of Arimathea, High Priest and First Patriarch of the Grail Family and Grail Priesthood impart understanding to the Peoples of the Grail, the three manifestations of the Grail Priesthood.

1—Know that the Angel Reysa has explained the first manifestations of the Divine Priesthood as it was from Adam to myself by way of the bloodline of Melchezedek, whoso was a Major God in the Celestial Realm and at times a Neutral Angel in the Terrestrial Realm.

2—And this was the first Divine Priesthood, and its secrets and mysteries were handed down from High Priest to High Priest.

3—And they guarded and protected the Divine Mystery of the Holy Grail, but did not hold it. And it was preserved and protected in the rites which held its mystery.

4—And this Divine Priesthood, which was known as the Melchezedek Priesthood performed the Divine Dispensations of teaching and preserving the mystery play (ritual allegory) of the Holy Grail. And they were empowered to Bless the Seekers of the Divine Mystery. The dead they did Bless, that they would live again to seek the Grail. They taught of the preexistence, and prepared mankind against the Luciferian Rebellion. And their teachings were both Wise and Divine.

5—The second manifestation of the Priesthood was with my son Jeshua the Teacher, he who is divine as he is also the son of T.G.A.O.T.U. and His Divine Princess Consort, Yse. That upon conception, T.G.A.O.T.U. did enter and possess me, and Yse did enter and possess Mary my wife. And our son, is Blessed to be both the son of the Divine First God and His Goddess Wife, and the son of a Terrestrial High Priest and High Priestess with a Royal Bloodline.

6—At this time, when Jeshua my son was of age, he became the first High Priest to impart further wisdom to the Divine Priesthood.

7—And he created the Priesthood to have 13 people, and he created the office of High Priestess, to be included in the Priesthood.

8—And thus, a High Priest would rule a Priesthood of a High Priestess and 11 disciples.

Book Two

1—And my son, the Divine Son, Jeshua the Teacher did well. But, the Luciferian Rebellion sought to murder him and destroy the High Priesthood.

2—And the Sanhedrin were called upon by Pilate, outside of their own laws to arrest and execute my Divine Son.

3—And they did this during the Passover, which was against their laws and traditions, and they arrested him and tried him and decided on an execution which was also unlawful according to their ways.

4—And I knew this land was no longer Holy, and was no longer the Chosen Land. And further with the help of my friend Nicodemus did bribe Pilate, that also against the laws of the Sanhedrin and the land and the laws of execution, we would save the life of Jeshua the Teacher that he would live for us. And against all laws of their land and their Priesthood, Jeshua would be crucified on my land in the garden of the tomb, which was against custom and law.

5—But, Jeshua would not die, but appear to die. That when

he thirsted, he would be given to inhale, not vinegar which would restore him, but be given in its stead a drug which would when inhaled, make him appear as dead.

6—And this was done. And I took the body and placed it in the tomb, which was also against custom and the laws of crucifixion.

7—And at the Place of the Skull, called Golgotha, Simon of Cyrene took the place of Jeshua the Teacher, and did so die for him in loyalty to the Holy Grail.

8—And now the Luciferian Rebellion thought they had won. And we sought to escape the land no longer Holy.

Book Three

1—And the Angel Erycina appeared unto me and told me that she would show me a new chosen land, but it would not be the last and final chosen land, but here we must escape and create the Third Manifestation of the Divine Priesthood, now to be called the Priesthood of the Holy Grail.

2—And the disciples were dispersed into the world to carry out the Dispensations of the Divine Priesthood.

3—And, I, Joseph, High Priest and Patriarch of the Grail Family took my wife Mary, and my son Jeshua, and Mary Magdala and Mary of Bethany any with the help of Nicodemus made our way to France.

4—And now, the Priesthood of the Holy Grail was confined to a family. And so, by Divine Dispensation, I made the First Grail Family into the First Grail Priesthood, and did give position and purpose to the 5 of the First Grail Family.

5—And I was to remain Grand Master, Jeshua the Teacher was to be the High Priest, and we were to represent the Two of Order. Mary, wife remained High Priestess, Mary of Bethany was made Handmaiden to her and Mary of Magdala was made

Grail Princess. And they were the Three of Chaos.

6—And together we were 5 being now a complete Priesthood, of the 2 of Order and the 3 of Chaos, being in perfect Balance.

7—By Divine Dispensation I Sealed all of us as a Divine Family, and Sealed our Positions as the Last Dispensation of the Positions of the High Priesthood, and the beginnings of the Bloodline.

8—And all after us would imitate this by their positions in the Priesthood.

9—And there would be 5 Principles of High Priesthood and there would be 8 disciples of lesser Priests and Priestesses.

10—And this High Priesthood would perform the Blessings and Divine Dispensations of Sealing, Initiation, Blessing the Dead, Teaching, the Eucharist and the allegorical Grail Rituals.

11—And there would be first, 3 degrees of Priesthood and above this there would be 5 Spiritual Degrees, and above this would there be 5 Royal Degrees. And this would be after the Divine Equation of the Holy Grail according to the Divine Mathematics of the Holy Grail.

12—And these equations by Divine Mathematics would become clear and known to the Grail Family during the Fullness of Times, when the Chosen Land, Chosen Language and Chosen Peoples would come together.

13—And by the Language and Divine Mathematics this sign would be made manifest. And at this end of times we would have to fight the Luciferian Rebellion as never before. And seek She who is as Yse incarnate.

Book Four

1—Here in this new Chosen Land would we make our family, and marry them to these Chosen Peoples who are the Celtic peoples.

2—And the children of my son Jeshua the Teacher were the first children of the Divine Bloodline of the First Family of the Holy Grail.

3—And in this new land he is called Joseph II or Joseph the Teacher.

4—The son of my son was born in this new land, and his mother, Mary of Magdala traveled full with child to this new land, and here he was born, and like his father he was light haired and blue eyed.

5—Unto Joseph the Teacher and Mary were there born 5 children. And they were two male children and three female children. And here the G.A.O.T.U. decreed by His Divine Dispensation and with the Sacred Blessing of Yse, She who is the Sacred Mother, that the males of this family, upon being taught and learned, should go secretly into the world and marry. And they should seek for marriage, only those women who have the Chosen Response of Yse in showing their love.

6—And the female children of this Sacred Family, have the same Blessing, but they should go openly into the world, and choose their husbands by showing their love through the Chosen Response of Yse, and he who accepts this way of woman, will be brought into the Sacred Family.

7—And she whose denies the Chosen Response is not of the Grail, though she may have the Bloodline.

8—And he who does not become illuminated at her Chosen Response of Love, will not be admitted into the Bloodline.

❁❁❁❁❁❁❁❁

Book Five

1—The son of my son (*Jeshua the Teacher*)was to be the Third Keeper of the Holy Grail, and he was to abide by the Sacred

Commandments given by the G.A.O.T.U. to the Divine Family. But he did not abide thereof, and he sought out the pleasures of common women and kept their company.

2—And my son, Joseph the Teacher, did take to anger, and he placed a curse upon his son. And this curse was to take the shape of the son having to live his many lives until She who was the Spirit of Yse would incarnate by chance and come across him and fall greatly in love with him and thus reveal the Chosen Response unto him as a sign of her love.

The Story of the Curse

I, Brons, will reveal the tragic and sad account of the Curse placed upon Joseph the Younger, by Jeshua the Teacher, also called Joseph the Teacher in this new land. It had been decreed by God that the First Divine Family escape the First Chosen Land and be removed unto the Second Chosen Land, there to establish the High Priesthood within the family and keep it by bloodline. And this task was fraught with obstacles and ordeals for the Divine Family, whose task it was to find husbands and wives for their grown children.

Those who were not yet prepared for the Royal Marriage, were bound to the study of the High Priesthood and turn away their lower passions. Yet they were encouraged to look for any who would make a suitable husband or wife, and enter the High Priesthood. And here, the Patriarch would test they who were chosen to wed, and be they found worthy, the wedding feast would be arranged.

And all were warned not to give in to the lower passions, but to seek only those men and women chosen by the Holy Grail, to keep company with and wed. Here and only here was it not against God and Yse for them to know the passions of their loins.

Yet, the son of Joseph the Teacher, being Joseph the Younger, in his 17th. year, was a High Priest of such a degree which had not ever been known before. And Joseph the First, had chosen him to be Keeper of the Holy Grail, after Joseph the Teacher.

Yet Joseph the Younger was a strong and vigorous man whose talents were many, and whose days were not long enough to fit therein all the tasks he would wish to undertake. And he was given to the lower passions and had been warned many a time never to stray from his duty to the High Priesthood and the Holy Grail.

After long hours of work with his father, he would rest a few hours with his companions, and they would drink and feast and discuss their trades, lives and the Priesthood.

And there came to the tavern where they often met, a girl of delightful beauty. And Joseph the Younger turned his attentions to her. And she was, by nature and instinct, of Yse, but had not been consecrated. And this she should have been, and he should have taken her to the Patriarch and the High Priesthood, and as I know, would have been consecrated as a Princess. But, Joseph did not act in wisdom but in folly. And he caused her to become big with child.

And when word of this reached Joseph the Teacher, he became angry, to the likes of which none had ever witnessed, and he vowed to curse his son for eternity. For not only had Joseph the Younger gone astray from his duty, but he had also ruined a girl who would have become a Princess if she had ever been consecrated.

For, now she was soiled by child, who, because she was not made a Princess, could not carry the bloodline.

And Joseph the Teacher cursed his son to walk his many lives without the love of a woman, to be bound to strict duty to the High Priesthood forever. And to the girl, he placed this curse, that none would desire her or love her, until she was possessed by the Spirit of Yse, and in another life found he who was once Joseph the Younger, and fell in love with him and return to him the Chosen Response. Whereby he would consecrate her and make her the Princess she was intended by God to be.

And knowing this curse to be harsh, but having no authority to put an end to it, Joseph the First created the First Ritual of the Grail Priesthood, which was the Marriage of the Elements. Herein, he would provide for Joseph the Younger, a manner in which the curse could be broken, as this Ritual contains all of the Mysteries of the Holy Grail. It is our Foundation Ritual, and therein be found the design to fulfil the Bargain of the Curse.

That being, Joseph the Younger never being allowed the love of a woman, that by this he is wounded in the genitals and never allowed to die. But he must incarnate and live for many lifetimes and search for Her who will cleave unto him with her love, and give him the Chosen Response. And Joseph the First, knowing this, created the Ritual of the Marriage of the Elements knowing that Joseph the Younger, in his many incarnations would serve the Grail Priesthood. And in so doing, would have the obligation to perform this ritual. And it being the only manner in which he would have the chance to kiss a woman. And herein, if she were to give him the Chosen Response upon being kissed, it would be as Yse, giving Her Response to Her Divine Husband, as a sign of Her love for Him.

And if such were to occur, the Bargain of the Curse would be fulfilled, and Joseph the Younger would be allowed to die. And then the Holy Grail could manifest at the feet of all females who are Pure of Heart, and the Wastelands will be restored. And at this time, the Luciferian Rebellion will be defeated and cease to have power.

(end of account)

3—And she would remove his curse, and this would not be made to manifest until the Fullness of Times, and they together would, by this act, please the G.A.O.T.U. and Yse, Divine Goddess of the Holy Grail. And the Grail would be restored to mankind and the Luciferian Rebellion overthrown, and Peace will come to the Terrestrial Realm.

4—And the son of my son was so wounded in the genitals, that he could neither breed, nor could he die. And upon the placing of the curse upon this family, the wife of Joseph the Teacher did take to her bed, and did there die.

5—And I, being the Patriarch of the family, yet the loving and understanding father of my son, Joseph the Teacher, did not oppose his decision. For it was prophesy as such in the pre-existence, when we were all Gods and Goddesses, that this would come to pass, and must be.

6—In the stead of going against the curse, I, Grand Master and Patriarch of the Divine Family of the Holy Grail and the High Priesthood of the Holy Grail, by authority granted unto me by the G.A.O.T.U. did decide to create a Rite of extreme importance. And that to, was Prophesy in the pre-existence. And this was pre-destined and agreed upon in the Celestial Realm as all is known which was, which is, and which will come to be.

7—And unto this I did create, through Divine Dispensation of the G.A.O.T.U. and Yse, Divine Goddess, by manner of Erycina, Neutral Angel and Major Goddess, a Sacred Rite, which could inspire the Chosen Response of Yse.

8—And that Rite would be known as the Marriage of the Elements, and it would invoke from the High Priestess or Princess of the Rite, that which is the Chosen Response of Yse. And here, in this rite, could the son of my son, in later lifetimes, within the High Priesthood have a chance to rid himself of the Grail Curse. That in performing the Sacred Kiss with the Grail Princess, there would be a chance that he might from her, receive the Chosen response. And she would love him deeply and by this Sacrifice of Love, overthrow the Luciferian Rebellion and restore Yse. And unto the world Her Spirit would be given.

9—And thus the son of my son, could not take his rightful place as the Third Keeper of the Holy Grail. And in the 12th. year after we came to this Second Chosen Land, my wife did give birth to the first daughter of this Sacred Family. And in her 13th. year, she was Sealed to Brons, the closest friend of my son, by the Royal Marriage.

10—After her mother, she too was named Mary. And by Divine Decree, I made Brons the Third Keeper of the Holy Grail. Their children were all sons, and they were 12. Here was the first family to descend from the First Family of the Grail. And unto them, Brons was Patriarch.

11—Alain, son of Brons, chose to remain virgin throughout his life, so by Divine Dispensation, I to him, did impart the Royal Secret, so that he could search the world for those females who held the Chosen Response, that they could be married unto his brothers. And this he did faithfully.

12—And this family carried the Grail. And Brons passed it to Joshua, his first son, and from Joshua the succession went unto Emondap, his first son.

13—Know, that here, is the Lineage of the Third Grail Keeper, from the Bloodline of the First Family.

Second Book of Joseph the Patriarch

Book One

1—According to the ways of the G.A.O.T.U. and Yse, Divine Goddess, and by the Divine Mathematics which hold the Secret of the Holy Grail, I Joseph, Grand Master and Patriarch of the Grail Priesthood, by authority of the Sacred Father and Divine Mother, did create Sacred Rites. And these Sacred Rites would hold, preserve and protect the Mysteries of Yse, being the Holy Grail.

2—And by Divine Dispensation, authority has been given unto me to set forth the positions of the High Priesthood and Lesser Priesthood, and to give each position its Divine Dispensation and Sacred Ordnance.

3—And first above all is the Grand Master and Patriarch, who is he who is the King who does not rule. Know that the Patriarch is Chosen directly by the G.A.O.T.U. And unto him are granted the Divine Dispensations of: Initiator, Teacher, Dispenser of Grail Law, Prophesy, Translation, Sealing, Authority and the duty to make Marriage Contracts with those of the Bloodline and High Priesthood.

4—And he, above all others is the communicator with the G.A.O.T.U., and he alone can translate these writings.

5—He will be the Highest of High Priests and possess the Degrees which are ours alone. And they be: 3 Physical Degrees, 5 Spiritual Degrees and 5 Spiritual Degrees.

6—And NONE come into the Order of the Holy Grail save through him, nor do they enter the Grail Family, save through his Patriarchal Blessing.

7—Unto the High Priest is the Summoner, who will assist him in his work, both within the High Priesthood and within matters which are of the Family of the Grail Bloodline. And he will be the communicator for the Royal Order and its Family.

8—And as the High Priest will represent the G.A.O.T.U. there shall be a special female in the Royal Hierarchy which will represent Yse. Divine and Sacred Goddess. And she will conduct herself as Yse in all her manner and disposition. And she shall have the Chosen Response. And she will be called Princess. And as the High Priest is Fire, the Grail Princess is Water.

9—And there shall also be a High Priestess who is also Water, and she will represent the Grail Females of the Terrestrial Realm, and communicate with Yse, through the Grail Princess.

10—Unto the High Priestess shall be a Grail Handmaiden, whoso is also Sacred to Water. And she shall assist the High Priestess.

11—And here be the 5 Principles of the Royal Hierarchy, who will serve to remind all yet to be born, of myself, Joseph of Arimathea—Patriarch and High Priest, Joseph the Teacher—Grail Keeper and Teacher, Mary of Magdala—Princess of the Holy Grail, Mary my wife—High Priestess and Mary of Bethany—Grail Handmaiden.

12—Each of these Principles are chosen according to their Illumination and their Works. And all will have no less than the 5th. Spiritual Degree, which is also the 8th. Degree.

13—And the High Priest and Summoner will be of Fire, and the Grail Princess, High Priestess and Grail Handmaiden will be of Water. Even unto avoiding fire and smoke in all manners. For any female whoso takes fire and smoke into her lungs is NOT of Water, and NOT of the Grail, even if she be born of the bloodline. And she whoso does take in fire and smoke and whose temperament is of fire, is of the Triple Headed Hecate and Lillith and acts under Lucifer and will be shunned and avoided. But, should she become Illuminated to these Laws, and change to obey them, she can then embrace Yse and be admitted into the Grail Priesthood and Family.

14—And there shall be also among the 5 Principals, 4 females who are Priestesses, who are of water and who will seek the Grail and she who, like them have the Chosen Response. And their honor will be to seek for the Princess whoso will break the curse on this Family.

15—And there will be 4 males who will be as Priests, and they will also seek the Grail and the Royal Princess.

16—And here the 8, thus Balance the 5 and create the 13. And this 8 will teach those who have made a Covenant with the Royal Order and they who seek the Holy Grail.

17—And each Temple will have a High Priest who will oversee the Temple and shall upon the power of T.G.A.O.T.U. and Yse. And he will open the Temple and close the Temple.

18—And he will give this power over to the Princess, for her to release that the Grail can be called upon to help the Priesthood. And together they will perform the Rite of the Marriage of the Elements. And the Grail Princess shall do all Blessings of the Temple and Priesthood.

19—And there shall be a Summoner, who will guard the Temple and go between Temples as a communicator.

20—And there shall be a High Priestess, whoso will prepare the Altar, all but light the flames.

21—And unto her will be a Handmaiden whoso will assist her in the Temple.

22—And the 8 others shall be Lesser Priests and Priestesses. And the Priestesses will also be Chantresses, whoso will sing the Litanys and Masses of the Holy Grail.

23—And the Rites will protect and teach the Mystery Plays of the Holy Grail. And here, those who wish to serve the Holy Grail and Quest for it, shall be admitted. And this be our Church which is hidden from the Luciferian Rebellion. Here, will be found the keys to the Quest, and the Grail Bloodline and entrance to the Grail Family.

❀❀❀❀❀❀❀❀

Book Two

1—Above all in importance is the Grail Princess, she who is of the spirit of Yse and is the Sacred Spring of the Holy Grail, and is thereof the Living Waters of the Holy Grail. That by her watery and gentle nature, she may attune to Yse at will and bring Her from the Celestial Realm unto the Terrestrial Realm to release the Living Waters of the Grail, which Bless, sanctify and purify.

2—She is Yse, and to seek to find Her, is to bring Yse, Sacred Goddess and the Lady of the Grail to the Terrestrial Realm, that she may be among us.

3—The 3 Physical Degrees are of the Grail Rites, litany's and masses, and the blessings and dispensations and ordnances as decreed by T.G.A.O.T.U. in the name of His love for Yse, Divine Goddess.

4—And these degrees are earthly and taught and learned and sanctified through initiation.

5—And the 5 Spiritual Degrees are, Quester, Protector, Guardian, Seeker and Holder. They are learned through illumination, and are confirmed and sanctioned only by the authority of the Patriarch.

6—The 5 Royal Degrees are the blessing of T.G.A.O.T.U. and Yse, Divine Goddess, and they are the keys to the activation and release of the powers of the Holy Grail. They are confirmed and sanctified by the Patriarch.

7—Those of the Royal Degrees know the meaning of the Quest, and now Quest for her who is the Grail Princess. And there may be many Grail Princesses, and one shall lift the Curse on the Grail Family and defeat the Luciferian Rebellion.

8—Know that within the High Priesthood and the Lesser Priesthood there are many peoples of many talents and gifts from T.G.A.O.T.U. and Yse, Divine Goddess. Know that the High

Priesthood and Lesser Priesthood are granted special Dispensations according to the nature of the Priest or Priestess after the third Physical Degree has been mastered. Here the Highest of High Priests who is the Patriarch and the Grail Princess will Bless and sanctify you with your Divine Dispensation given freely from T.G.A.O.T.U. and Yse, Divine Goddess. And they be; Blessing of the dead, to ease the passing of the dying from this life to the next. Sealing of friends and family, which binds them together for all time and eternity. Royal Marriage Sealing, which Seals a man and a woman together for all time and eternity. Bequests, which are Blessings for the sick, hungry, oppressed, homeless and the like.

Book of Amberis

Book One

WHEREUPON the Neutral Angel Amberis did impart unto Joseph of Arimathea certain particulars concerning the Grail Princess.

1—To Her who is a Grail Princess, know that all of what you have been told by my sisters and brothers will be familiar. And unto Her, understanding and meaning in life will be Her Great Gift.

2—And She will be protected from the harm of evil, so long as She does not falter from her purpose in life. For Hers is a great purpose, and she is onto a Goddess upon the earth.

3—And She will have come home by way of these teachings, and they will set Her apart from the rest of the Female Race.

4—And when She has discovered the Mysteries and Secrets of the Holy Grail, and unmasked their riddle, neither confirm nor deny Her answer, but, let Her be further tested by Her faith.

5—And in secret, have the Highest High Priestess prepare Her Spiritually and Physically. Take care that She knows Herself and is content with the Mystery She has uncovered. Take care that She can prove the answer to the riddle.

6—And upon Her Spiritual Illumination being confirmed by the Highest High Priest and the Highest High Priestess, the Highest High Priestess must prepare Her for Initiation into the Royal Degrees, And here, Her body will be Ritually Washed, Cleansed and Scented, that She will be made opposite to Lillith in body and spirit, and pledge to this way stay for all time, as Her declaration of Her faith, and that She may be known and recognized as a Grail Princess.

7—And She will be dressed in the garment of a Princess and the robe of a Princess. And this shall be done by authority of the Highest High Priestess and her Priestesses.

8—And She will prepare Herself with prayers to Yse, Divine Goddess of the Holy Grail. And She will devise a Blessing for the Highest of High Priests and Highest of High Priestess, and so Bless them with the life of salt and water. And they in turn will Bless Her in the name of the G.A.O.T.U. and Yse, Divine Goddess of the Holy Grail. And they will celebrate the Royal Eucharist together.

Book Two

WHEREUPON Amberis imparted unto Joseph of Arimathea, details of Grail Families and how they are determined.

1—Jeshua the Teacher was the begotten son of the G.A.O.T.U., for at his conception did the G.A.O.T.U. come into you as the chosen earthly father, and did Yse possess Mary as the earthly mother.

2—Thus, Jeshua the Teacher is wholly Divine as he has within him both the blood of the First God and First Goddess and the blood of the First Chosen earthly Father and Mother.

3—And from the bloodline of Jeshua the Teacher, comes the bloodline of the G.A.O.T.U. and Yse, Divine Goddess. And from that bloodline comes the Purest Grail Princess and the Purest High Priests.

4—And from your other 4 children comes the lineage, whereupon the mysteries of the Holy Grail are founded.

5—Know that a Grail mother may teach and impart to her daughter the ways of a Princess, but this may not be imparted to a son by either the mother or the father. And the sons must discover the riddle for themselves.

6—A pure Grail female MUST marry a pure Grail male, and a pure Grail male must marry a pure Grail female.

7—For as Grail females go openly into the world they must only marry males who recognize their element. And as Grail males go secretly into the world they must seek only Grail females whose element they recognize. And here, the Bloodline and Lineage is preserved for the greater good, against the Luciferian Rebellion.

8—There is both the bloodline and the lineage of the family. And those who will descend from the house of Jeshua the Teacher, are descendants of the G.A.O.T.U. and Yse, Divine Goddess, and they are Pure to the Holy Grail. And they are of the Ancient Race of the Pre-Existence, and all of their females are of Yse and bear the Chosen Response.

9—And those whoso be descended from the house of Joseph of Arimathea are the chosen peoples and by birth may lay claim to their lineage for it is also the birthright of those who have been separated from the Grail Family to come back unto the family.

10—Marriage into the bloodline or lineage does not mean that you become of the blooodline or Lineage, but thereof, your children will so be.

11—And that She with the Chosen Response, who is chosen by a Grail male for marriage will be brought before the Patriarch and he will determine if she is of the Bloodline or Lineage, for she who bears the Chosen Response of Yse, Divine Goddess, can not be other than the Bloodline or the Lineage, save for she who is so gentle and pure, that she sacrifices herself by leaving the race of common man, and becoming devoted to the Holy Grail and Yse. by discovering and cherishing the Chosen Response of Yse. And she will be equally loved by the peoples of the Grail Family, which is a race, akin to mankind, but also of the Heavens.

12—A female child may be taken into the Grail Family, if she has no family of her own and taught the ways of Yse, by her new mother. And should she find comfort in these ways, she shall have them as her right. And she will become married to a Grail male and their children will be Grail.

13—But, if she does not find comfort in the ways of Yse, she shall be given over to family not of the Grail.

14—And a male child may be taken in, but not taught the ways of Yse, or her secret. And should he not discover or accept the Great Secret, he will be married off to she who is not of the Grail, but, if he discovers and accepts the Secret of Yse, he shall be married off to a Grail Female and their children will be Grail.

15—Only he who has mastered the Royal Degrees, and who has come to discover and accept the ways of Yse, Divine Goddess, shall he marry only she who is of Yse, and who has the Chosen Response. For if he marry she who is not of Yse, for the sake of love-lust and not the Grail, he will be cut off from the Bloodline and Lineage, and will curse his children as they will not be born Grail.

16—And thusly, she who bears the Chosen Response will not be permitted to marry he who is ignorant of its meaning. She will not be cut off, but she will be made Lesser. And if she has female children and imparts to them the ways of the Chosen Response of Yse, she will be restored unto the family, and the female children will be Grail, and over them will be the Grandfather and Grandmother in their teaching. For here the father will serve for nothing, save if he comes to discover and accepts the Grail.

17—She who is Perfect and Pure in Yse, and bears the Chosen Response is required to marry he who is a High Priest and Holds the Grail. And only they may be Sealed in Marriage for Time and Eternity. And they may not become separated in life.

18—The age for a female of the Grail to be married is 13

years, as she may bear children at this time. And she must be trained by her mother and the other High Priestesses in the ways of Yse, Divine Goddess, and in the ways of the husband, the children and the home.

19—The age of a male to marry is 17 years when he has mastered a Trade and can feed, clothe and house his wife and family.

20—And at times it is best to tend the custom of the land concerning marriage according to age and caste.

21—And those females who are Grail Princesses shall have the duty to arrange meetings of males and females for marriage. And they will choose each other also in love, as well as the importance of the Bloodline and Lineage of the Grail.

22—The Bloodline and Lineage comes through the men of the Grail Peoples, and is kept Pure through the Grail females. And upon marriage, the Grail female takes the name of the husband, and then comes unto his family.

23—And whereupon the Grail Female bears the Chosen Response, and the husband honors his wife for her bond unto Yse, this marriage and family will be doubly blessed and belong to both his family and her family.

❁❁❁❁❁❁❁❁❁❁❁

Book Three

WHEREUPON the Angel Amberis did impart unto Joseph, the details and duties of the husband, wife, children and family.

1—A male becomes a man when he has mastered a Trade and can provide for his wife a house, clothing and food. And a female becomes a woman, upon having her courses and learning the ways of the home, the husband and the children.

2—And the wife teaches the female children in her ways and the husband teaches the male children in his Trades.

3—And there shall come a time when the children will reach an age whereupon their minds will be distracted by their loins. And they will forsake their duties to both the father and the mother, in favor of that new desire which compels young males and young females to seek one another that their pangs of joy may be released.

4—And it is the duty of the mother to see fit that the daughter does not swell big with child, and to give her daughter remedy against this. And if the daughter does swell big with child, it is also the duty of the mother to see fit that the child is never born. And should its birth be not halted, it will be given unto the mother of the daughter to raise until the daughter is set to marry. And then she shall take the child and care for it. And these are the ways of daughters and mothers and their ways alone, which are not unto the males or men or fathers.

5—And much care must be taken when a young female and a young male play, about their pangs of joy which their loins cry out to be spilt. And they must be allowed to have such play, amid the laughter and jests of the older males and females whoso will council them in the ways of these simple pleasures.

6—And know that when a young male or young female comes of marriageable age and grows to feel these pangs of joy and there is none of their age to have play with and spill them and give release from their distraction, it may be arranged that a Setore or a Satora will be chosen to initiate and satisfy them and be at their call, ever ready to satisfy their pangs.

7—Know that at this age, the desires of the loins may also create a desire of the head, and the desire of the head is not real, but an illusion. Take care that the young females and the young males do not take up with others who are of divers religions. Know that they must only cavort in play with those of their own Bloodline and Lineage.

8—Know that if any young male is deemed ready for marriage by the father and the High Priesthood, know that he must marry within the Bloodline and Lineage. And that if he marries another who is outside the Bloodline and Lineage, the Bride will be instructed by the High Priestesses and Princesses and the mother of the Groom in the ways of the Grail. And if a young female chances to marry outside the Bloodline and Lineage, her groom will be instructed in the ways of the Grail by the High Priesthood and her father.

9—And here the outsiders will be judged after one year and one day, as to their worthiness to marry one of the Grail. And if judged so worthy they will marry in the way of the Grail.

10—Know that all outsiders will relinquish their former religions if they are to marry into the Grail Family, even if it means to be shunned by their natural family.

11—And any who marry outside the Grail, and choose love-lust above their duty will be shunned and banished.

12—Know also that she whoso is young, may marry he who is old, and as such, he who is young may marry she who is old. And be they Grail by Bloodline or Lineage, it will be a good and blessed marriage. And know that any whoso come into a Grail Marriage have the Blessing of the G.A.O.T.U. and Yse upon their children.

13—Teach your children that the love of the loins is good, but the love of the heart is a compliment to the love of the loins, and the love of the head is but folly.

14—The inheritance of wealth upon the death of the father is bequeathed firstly in the greatest part to the eldest son, if he is of the Royal Degrees. And be he not, its greatest part goes to the second eldest son who is of the Royal Degrees & etc. And the rest is divided between the remaining children. Know that the greatest part is one half of the wealth of the father. The remaining one half is divided amongst the rest of the children. Know that inheritance is also to be divided according to those children who have entered the Royal Degrees. And if a daughter be a Perfect Grail Princess, she shall inherit a larger part.

And this will be decided upon by the High Priesthood.

15—And there is no greater gift that a wife can give her husband, than that of a daughter whoso is a Grail Princess. And she will be cherished above all.

16—And each daughter will be trained as a Perfect Grail Princess, and be shown all the keys and riddles from the High Priestesses and the Princesses, and the mother if she is such.

17—Each mother whoso is a Grail Princess and of the Royal Degrees will instruct her daughters to be Grail Princesses. And she, whoso has a daughter and she herself is not a Princess, shall give her daughter over for training to a Grail Princess, and thus the family shall be blessed from upon high.

18—And the mother shall instruct her daughters in the Sacred Duty of being a mother. And she shall teach her of the home and its importance and the importance of children and the celebration of the family and its peace and joy when they feast together. And she shall teach her daughter of the manner in which the home is made content, and of her purpose as a female of the Grail Bloodline and Lineage.

19—The father shall teach his son his Trade and make him a Master. And the son may seek out other apprenticeships in other Trades, that he will be able to keep the family fed, warm, housed, clothed and content.

20—Upon marriage, the husband and the wife will be also close in companionship as friends. And this shall teach the children. And they shall love each other in the heart, which shall teach the children. And they shall teach each other in the loins, which will be apart from the children, and unto them only.

21—And the home is the province of the wife and daughters, and the husband and sons shall not partake in the duties of the home such as the making and mending of clothes, preparing of food, save for the making of the fire or raising and caring of children, for this demands the Gentle Nature of the mothers and daughters.

22—And the trade is the responsibility of the husband and the sons, and by work of the Trade, the family will survive, and it is all important for their food, clothing, shelter, warmth and happiness.

23—That which is the dominion of the wife, will not demand the attention of the husband. And that which is the dominion of the husband will not demand the attention of the wife. Know this and know it well, for it is the foundation of the family. Those duties which are set forth for the female are her duties alone, and those duties of the male are his. And to cross them will bring ruin to the family. And this is the way it was in the Celestial Realm during the time of the pre-existence, and must be the Natural Order upon the Terrestrial Realm.

❀❀❀❀❀❀❀❀

Book Four

1—Know that there be those husbands and their wives who are great companions and whose play with each other is as the young males and young females. And ofttimes they choose not to raise families, but may work together for the Grail and its Bloodline and Lineage. And know that in the manner of living, the wife may help the husband in his Trade. Know also and well, that it is their bond which makes them this way. But, she must NEVER become as the Nature of a Man in this manner of living, but must always hold on to her nature as a Priestess of Yse.

2—And these peoples are Wanderers who travel unto divers kingdoms in Quest for the Grail and the Sacred and Royal Princesses.

3—Know that they are the Esarne (Wanderers and Questers), whose duty it is to Quest for the Grail, Seek the Sacred Princesses and seek those who have become lost from the Bloodline and Lineage and bring them together.

4—And those of the Bloodline and Lineage will render help to any of their people if so asked. And they will take in and feed, shelter, protect and give sanctuary without question or payment.

5—And none who are Grail will refuse to help any other who is Grail. And when a family suffers the ills of poverty, the Grail peoples will gather and provide for them a house, food, clothing and enough wealth for the husband to build his trade. And this they will do freely, for here, there will be another family whoso will return the gift of help to those who will be in need in their time of trouble.

6—And if a wife leaves a husband and family for another man who is not of the Bloodline and Lineage, she shall be shunned, and none will help her. And this law also is for a husband if he so leaves his wife and family.

7—And no wife, if she leaves her husband for another man, shall take her children, for they are first of the Grail and she can not deprive them of their birthright. And she will be cut off from the Grail, the family, the Bloodline and the Lineage.

8—And the children will be turned over to the sisters of the husband and they to care for the children until he can a wife find. And then he shall take possession of his children.

9—Children of the father and mother will live with their family until they are married. And they shall only leave the home and family unmarried to seek a companion in marriage. And the men will leave in secret and never reveal their true names or lineage. And the women will leave and go into the world openly, and they will be recognized by Grail men and be chosen to marry.

10—And then they will return to the home and a wedding feast will be prepared according to custom. And both the family of the bride and groom will unite and recognize each other.

11—And the children of the family shall take care of the elders of the family. Thus the father and the mother raise and teach the children, and when they are old, the children for them do care, feed, clothe and shelter.

12—Beware pretenders to the Grail, for they are of the Luceferian Rebellion. And they will make their claims in boast, and they will make great claims upon the knowledge, wisdom and understanding of the Grail, yet they will know nothing and not be able to prove themselves. And they will Covet any female thought to be a Grail Princess, and her they will deprive of the truth of the Grail, and her Destroy In Spirit.

13—For if these Pretenders were of the Grail, even unto distant ancestry, they would not merely covet degrees and make loud boasts, and they would not go against the Doctrine of the Grail and destroy the Spirit of and female who may be of Yse. But they would send her to the High priesthood and wish her to be Tested and Trained to enter the High Priesthood. For none shall Covet a Grail Princess, for it is her right and duty to live unto Yse and serve the Holy Grail, as she was chosen to do. And those who would keep her from the High Priesthood, Bloodline and Lineage, are of the Greatest Evil, and work not for the Grail, but against it in all their manner of work.

Book Five

1—Those of the Grail Bloodline and Lineage must only marry within their own people. And they must receive the Blessing of the High Priesthood to do so.

2—If one, of the Grail wishes to marry outside the Bloodline and Lineage, the outsider must forsake their religion and philosophy and take up that which is of the Grail. Or the marriage will not be recognized or be sanctioned by the High Priesthood or family.

3—And, if one of the Grail marries outside the Grail and does not take their birthright into the family, by conversion of their chosen mate, there children will be deprived of their birthright. And they, who were of the Grail, will be shunned and banished and the Rites of the Dead will be said for them, for to the Bloodline and Lineage they will be as dead. But they will also be as a murderer, for they will have stripped their children of their birthright, which is their life.

4—They who are to be married will be brought before the High Priesthood and given the Blessing of T.G.A.O.T.U. and Yse, Sacred Goddess.

5—And be they of the Royal Degrees, they shall each be given a gift: Unto the groom will be given 2 golden bees, which represent T.G.A.O.T.U. and Yse, Sacred Goddess. And unto the bride shall be given 3 golden bees, and they shall represent Jeshua ben Jusef, being Jeshua the Teacher, Mary of Magdala and Mary of Bethany.

Book Six

1—The Grail Marriage is the most Sacred and Royal Wedding. It is the only Marriage upon the Terrestrial Realm which is Blessed by the G.A.O.T.U. and Yse, Divine Goddess, for it is as Their Marriage, which is Sacred above All.

2—The Royal Marriage of the Holy Grail is a Sacred Sealing of a man and a woman for all Time and Eternity, whose Seal can not be broken.

3—For Five days before the Wedding Rites, she who will be Bride is attended by the Sacred Princesses and High Priestesses, and her body is ritually prepared as a Princess. And she is ritually dressed.

4—And she shall go into a consecrated room and there stay for 5 days and be attended to by the Sacred Princesses and High Priestesses. And there she will study the ways of the Grail and be in communion with Yse, Sacred and Divine Goddess.

5—And on the Fifth day she will be Ritually Bathed and her body scented and prepared by the Sacred Princesses and High Priestesses and be brought to the place of the wedding.

6—Three days after she enters the consecrated chamber, the groom to be shall also be led to a consecrated chamber where he will study the Doctrine of the Holy Grail and the people of the Bloodline and Lineage for the space of two days, attended by the Sacred Princesses and High Priestesses. On the second day, he will have his beard shaven and be dressed for the wedding and brought to the place of the wedding.

7—And here, the High Priest and the Sacred Princesses will oversee the Wedding Rites, and Bless the union of the bride and the groom. And this Sacred Rite is performed only in the presence of the bride, groom, High Priest, Sacred Princesses and High Priestesses.

8—After the Sacred Rite of the Royal Marriage is performed, the Wedding Feast will be celebrated and last for the space of 3 days. And here the husband and wife shall be given gifts of money, jewels, gold, silver and spices, that they may have wealth for their family. And there shall be much food and drink for all, given freely by the families of the bride and the groom. And there shall be much dancing and music and rejoicing during this celebration. And each day at sunrise, shall prayers be said to the G.A.O.T.U. and Yse to open the day, and again at sunset, shall prayers of thanks be said to close the day.

❁❁❁❁❁❁❁❁

Book Seven

1—The birthing of children shall be attended to by the Sacred Princesses and the High Priestesses and Priestesses. And be it that a female child is born, she will be Blessed by the Sacred Princesses, that she may grow to become a Sacred and Divine Princess of the Holy Grail.

2—Be it a male child that be born, he will be Blessed by the High Priests that he may grow to learn the Royal Degrees.

3—And this is the domain of women, and no male shall be present. But after the birth, the father may sit with the mother.

4—And the Sacred Princesses and High Priestesses will tend the mother and child for 5 days, and then she may leave her bed.

5—The Soul enters the body of the child when the birth string is cut. For in one body, two souls can not dwell. And that Soul which chooses the child, comes unto the mother as it senses the conception. And there may be many souls around her which will fight to enter and inhabit the child. And that Soul which is true for the child, is that which has been Sealed to that Soul of the Mother, and it will win over the others and go into the child upon the severing of the Birth String. And at this severing the Sacred princess shall say the Prayer of Birthing. The mother shall be protected with Prayers, said by the Sacred Princesses and High Priestesses at the full of every moon, from the first month that she is big with child. And this shall be done so the souls which surround her and fight for entry to possess the child do not confuse and upset the Spirit and Mind of the mother.

Book Eight

1-Upon death, the High Priests of the Dead will wash and annoint the body and wrap it in a linen shroud, and also prepare the body with cinnamon, cloves, allspice, frankincense and myrrh. And they shall prepare a tomb scented with incense and the burnings of fragrant herbs. And the body therein shall be laid.

2—And also therein shall be contained a scroll with the name and lineage of the deceased and the Death Prayers of the deceased.

3—And this shall be done by the Priests of the Dead who are celibate and never allowed to touch a female or be married, for their dominion is the dead, and not the living.

4-And the High Priest shall say the Mass of the Dead, and read the words of the deceased, which are the Death Prayers. And they describe the place that the Spirit of the body will create for himself in the Tellestial Realm. And the High Priest shall help the Spirit of that body attain the surroundings of his reward in the Tellestial Realm, and call upon those who have before him died, that unto him were Sealed that they may be with each other.

5—And the families, friends and companions will gather for 5 days and give unto each other comfort. And they shall feast and drink and talk of the deceased, that he will be remembered and his life shared with all. And they shall bring gifts of wealth to help the family. And the family shall be cared for, for 8 months, here to being given comfort. And during this space of time the family will have grieved.

Book of Therac

WHEREUPON the Neutral Angel, Therac did impart unto Joseph of Arimathea, signs which will mark the Fullness of Times.

1—Know and teach your people that the Purpose of Life is to Quest for the Holy Grail, that we may restore it to the Celestial Realm, and there we may return as Gods and Goddesses and know the Balance of Order and Chaos.

2—Know well that for each of the peoples of the Grail there are those of the Luciferian Rebellion and those controlled by the Luciferian Rebellion who would thwart our plan and steal away from us the Grail and deprive mankind of its gift. And we would then live in suffering and even upon return though we return as Gods and Goddesses, we would not know the Balance of Order and Chaos, and all would be imbalanced, and life would be no better than the hardships we have in the Terrestrial realm.

3—And know that the war to possess the Holy Grail is great. And that in the Fullness of Times there will be certain signs which will be shown to your descendants, and these signs will mark the Fullness of Times, and if then we can possess the Grail and keep it from the Luciferian Rebellion, the Balance of Order and Chaos will come upon the Terrestrial Realm.

4—And its sign will be marked by peace, plenty, health, happiness and love. And this will replace war, strife, poverty, floods, drought, illness and famine. And all evils will be wiped from the Terrestrial Realm.

5—In the Fullness of Times, more rare than precious gems will be those females who are possessed by Yse, who are the Grail Princess. And the more rare the Grail Princess becomes, the more the Luciferian Rebellion will take life from Yse, Divine and Sacred Goddess, and be that they vanquish, she will cease to exist, and both the Terrestrial Realm and the Celestial Realm will be thrown into Chaos.

6—That to protect and hold the Holy Grail is to restore life to Yse, Sacred and Divine Goddess.

7—And females not of the Grail, but who serve the dark and evil Goddess of the Luciferian Rebellion, whoso is called Lillith, whoso be the hairy fiend of the night, she whoso caused the First Luciferian Rebellion by tempting the Tribe of Adam by way of her evil influence over the Tribe of Eve, will again wrought her evil over females.

8—And she will turn her females and common females against the females of the Grail, and she will cause men to go as women and women to go as well. And here, she who is most evil above all other evil, will cause men to incarnate as women and women to incarnate as men, that she may have her hold over them. But, many that she would hold will reject her and return to their right incarnations as they were in the pre-existence, be they then Gods, then men they shall return as. And be they Goddesses, then women they shall return as.

9—And she shall cause women to think themselves, by that which is unto them natural, filthy. And unto them she will impart this idea that the female body and its natural functions, courses and odour are against society and should be hidden as they are shameful. And this is against Yse, Sacred and Divine Goddess above all other Goddesses. For through Yse, that which is unique to her body and of the watery element is sacred and special to all females, and should not be hidden for there is no shame to these things, save to she who has shame in her soul.

10—And it is hurtful and against Yse to find shame in these things and to hide them in shame, for they are natural and define her Sacred Race.

11—And to females, Lilith will steal from them water, and

instill them with fire that they will destroy their own nature. And they will not know what they do, but feel that to be fiery is their way. And they shall be entrapped. For they know not that she is their greatest enemy.

12—And in the Fullness of Times, the Sacred and Divine Mathematics of the Holy Grail will manifest in the Chosen Language, and therein all elements of the Holy Grail will be taught, shown and proven to the peoples of the Holy Grail. And here, the Luciferian Rebellion under Lilith, will even try to change the chosen language to thwart the Holy Grail.

13—And there will be one more Chosen Land, from this one. And the Chosen Land will be marked by the Chosen Language, and further it will be marked by that land where all will travel unto, even if the journey is filled with danger. And this is the Third and Final Chosen Land, and here, all tongues will be forsaken for the Chosen Language. And to our people this land will be sacred, and all who are of the Bloodline and Lineage and who have embraced the Holy Grail have Divine Right to live in the Third Chosen Land, as it is a land bound together for freedom where we can live openly, and the number of the Chosen Land is 5. For here there is Balance.

Book of Varena

Book One

WHEREBY she, who is the Spirit of Yse visited unto Joseph of Arimathea and imparted unto him the ways of Yse, and they who are the Sacred Royal Princesses of the Holy Grail.

1—I am the Spirit of Yse who walks among women and imparts unto them their Sacred Duty unto the Holy Grail.

2—I am love and gentleness and innocence and purity and passiveness and self sacrifice. My duty is great, and without me, all would perish. I am the Spirit within all females which allows them to Hold the Holy Grail, and without my Blessed Spirit, no female can hold the Grail.

3—My way is purity and contentment and passive strength. She who is of me is without malice, or scorn, or hatred, or meanness, or grudge, or revenge, or defiance or aggression.

4—Know that I am the handmaiden of Yse, Divine Goddess, and that I chose the 3 Mary's to inhabit as they accepted me. And that I will accept any female whoso accepts me, and as they are of me, I am of them.

5—Know that my name is Sacred and Divine unto Yse. And I am the rain of Yse which binds all females to the Earth.

6—Know that I am water, and not fire.

7—Hidden within my name is the Divine Equation as well as 'one', which represents she who accepts me.

8—Know that she who embraces my name, is Sacred, and unto her will I impart the ways of Yse, and she may have the honor of removing the curse upon the Fisher King and the Grail Family.

Book Two

1—She will accept it at 5. She will know it at 8. To her it will be natural at 13. At 17 it will be her attraction. At 23 it will be part of her.

2—For she whoso is of me, is of Yse, who is Divine Goddess, and who brings Water to Earth by Salt. And these are the 3 Elements of a female who is Truly Sacred.

3—And know her by her Sacred Garment, which tells of her Divinity and Sacredness.

4—And many will oppose her and bear malice towards her. But through her innocence and purity and passiveness shalt she find strength without Fire.

5—For only she has the Divine Dispensation to Bless and Consecrate. And only she can Hold the Holy Grail, for only she is Pure, and has won the favor of Yse.

Book Three

1—I can be recognized by who I am, and that is gentleness, purity, innocence and passiveness, and as such I am the Divine Feminine.

2—I am Water and have no part of Fire, for I am the Spirit of Yse, Sophia Divine.

3—I am within the girl child of innocence. I am within the young woman ready for love as passiveness. I am within she who is wanting in love, as gentleness. I am within she who is big with child, as purity. I am all of these things in the Sacred Princess as femininity, for she holds them all. I am she who unites water, salt and earth when kissed by fire and air.

4—She whoso receives my blessing is Sacred amongst females. And she is both born unto me, or is chosen and comes unto me.

5—And her Sacred Duty is to contain Yse, and bring her among mankind, and it is to remove the Grail Curse in the Fullness of Times, and she will be Blessed above all.

❁❁❁❁❁❁❁❁

Book Four

1—And when Jeshua the Teacher did curse his son Joseph the Younger, was I called upon to help mankind. That I should enlighten all females to Sacredness.

2—And I came after the Neutral Angels, from Yse, Her Spirit and Gift to all females.

3—Into each and every female I would dwell, knowing that many would reject me and few would accept me.

4—And my purpose would be to give myself to the First and Last Son of Jeshua the Teacher, that I would remove his burden.

5—And by this Act of Sacrifice, would all change, and all would receive the Blessing of the G.A.O.T.U. and Yse. And Lucifer, Lillith and the Triple Headed Hecate will be overthrown and Michael will not have acted in vain.

❁❁❁❁❁❁❁❁

Book Five

1—And she whoso is of me, will find Strength in her Weakness.

2—And she shall be known by the Mystery and Riddle that she will Bind Water, Salt and Earth as one, when she is Kissed by Fire and Air.

3—She will know herself to be special and strive to prove

herself.

4—And unto her is all Beauty, for she is of Yse. Yet her clothes be rent and soiled, she is pure beauty, and Divine Feminine.

5—And she will be challenged with her own duty, yet her own thought will pass unto that duty, even beyond herself. And through her, all mankind will find peace and freedom, through her Sacrifice of Love.

Second Book of Varena

Book One

WHEREUPON Varena, the Spirit of Yse spoke unto Joseph regarding the signs of the Fullness of Times when the Luciferian Rebellion will manifest its tools.So endeth the Lesser Book of the Holy Grail.

1—There will occur, certain and specific signs and omens which will show the power of the Luciferian Rebellion. And these signs and omens will show that the Luciferian Rebellion is growing in its strength.

2—And by these signs, know that Evil is upon the world and that it seeks to destroy the Holy Grail. And it seeks to bring Chaos to the Terrestrial Realm, and to destroy Yse, Sacred and Divine Goddess. And even unto common women will, they to be destroyed by being deprived of their Natural Instincts.

3—Read these signs in the Third and final Holy Land, where the Chosen People will settle. Know that this will occur, and here the Chosen Language is a Key, and even here will the agents of Lillith and the Triple Headed Hecate even try to destroy the Chosen Language.

4—The Third Chosen Land will be won through War, for Freedom, and to escape the tyranny of the Second Chose Land. And here, these who fight are the First Chosen People, and they will build the land and Create its Customs and Traditions.

5—And these peoples will come from the Second Chosen Land, and leave their homes for the Freedoms and Chances the Third Holy Land will promise. And these are the First Chosen Peoples, and their Descendants are also the Chosen People.

6—And in later times, when the land is settled and built,

there will be those from the First and Second Chosen Lands, who shall come as thieves in the night. And they will usurp the Customs and traditions of the Third Chosen Land.

7—For they shall be drawn by the Greatness of the Third Chosen Land and covet that which is the Dominion of the Chosen Peoples. Yet they will not take on the Customs and traditions, yea, they will even forsake the Chosen Language.

8-And they are NOT the descendants of the Chosen Peoples.

9—And the Chosen Peoples will reject them, as they will be found to be thieves. And they will rob the Chosen Peoples of their Trades, and land, and homes and food.

10—And in these times shall the Chosen Language be attacked and degraded by the Luciferians, and they shall be under Lillith, the Hairy Demoness and the Triple Headed Hecate.

11—And they shall strike from the language all references to the Great Architect, by way of removing him from the language. And this they shall do by attacking peoples to strip them of their God and Goddess spirits, making them as each other, without reference to their sex.

12—and they will strive to change the Chosen Language, which will cause confusion. and this is to destroy the prophesy of the Holy Grail. For its prophesy and the ways of Yse are revealed and proven through the divine Mathematics of the Holy Grail, set down in the Celestial Realm by T.G.A.O.T.U. and they will try and destroy those words which describe a Sacred and Divine Princess, which contain the Sacred equations. And make these words vile unto females. And here know the females who are of Lucifer, Lilith and the Triple Headed Hecate, for they will hate the Princess words.

13—And the Weak Willed and Self Willed will be sought by Lucifer, Lillith and the Triple Headed Hecate, and they will be guided towards the Destruction and Imprisonment of their own Souls. And they shall be as Pawns to the Luciferian Rebellion as they will be guided to destroy the Land and the Language.

14—And here they shall bend the minds of the people to their Foul and Stinking Wills. And thus create a great War betwixt Men and Women.

15—They shall create and change customs at Will, that they may lead the Weak of Spirit and Self Willed. And they shall be used for evil purposes and ends. They shall take what was once one thing, and define it as another that they may create guilt and incite slander and false witness between families and men and women. And they will give their False Doctrine the appearance of Fact, by their Evil Influence over the Weak Willed and Self Willed. For they will only see a tool to hurt and feel the Luciferian Power, by creating Lies, Slander and False Witness. And this will hurt and destroy many innocent lives.

16—And here, up will become down, and down become up. And the Weak of Spirit and Weak Minded shall believe their False Doctrine.

17—And here shall be introduced the Age of Chaos and Confusion. And this shall mark the Fullness of Times. And here Free Will and Choice will cease, for to reject the Holy Grail is to be Chosen to Serve the Luciferian Rebellion.

So endeth the Lesser Book of the Holy Grail, also called The Merovingian Bible

About the Authors

Joseph of Arimathea, author of *The Book of the Holy Grail*, was the father of Jeshua ben Jusef, commonly known as Jesus. He was a High priest of the Melchezedek priesthood. When Jeshua was conceived, the Great Architect of the Universe came into Joseph, and Yse came into Mary, his wife. Thus, Jeshua was born of the bloodline of God and man. Joseph of Arimathea was visited by the Neutral Angels and given the Grail Doctrine in the year 54 A.D. He wrote *The Book of the Holy Grail* for the High Priesthood and his descendants.

J.R. Ploughman, author of *Keys to the Quest*, by right of inheritance and lineage, is a very private person, being the current Patriarch of the Merovingian Gnostic Church, Order of the Holy Grail, and the current Grand Master of the Strict Observance—Knights Templar/Illuminati, The United Orders of the American Rite. He is married to a Grail Princess and has two sons, Edward 16 and Reginald 11 months. J.R. has been a writer and publisher of rare esoteric books since 1975. He is a staunch libertarian and defender of First and Second Amendment rights. He has written, published and edited many traditional magickal books as well as penned some Discordian/Erisian texts of bombastic humor. His current and most engrossing project is his band, Cat Chaser Conspiracy, a blend of punk, goth, and babydoll music.

Thomas Jefferson, the original translator of *The Book of the Holy Grail* into English, was born April 13, 1743, in Virginia, which he called home for most of his life, serving as its governor and authoring its Declaration of Rights. Jefferson was also the primary author of the American Declaration of Independence in 1776. Thomas Jefferson served as governor of Virginia, a congressman, minister to France, secretary of state, and the third President of the United States. In addition to his political career, he was a lawyer, a classical scholar and linguist, a musician, a farmer and horticulturist, an inventor, and an architect, as well as having been Grand Master of the Strict Observance—Knights Templar, The United Orders of the American Rite. In addition to his translation of *The Book of the Holy Grail,* Jefferson also edited his own version of the traditional Judeo-Christian Bible from textual sources in several languages. One of Thomas Jefferson's most famous statements, inscribed on the Jefferson Memorial in Washington D.C., is, "I have sworn upon the altar of God eternal hostility against every form of tyranny over the mind of man." He died July 4, 1826, the 50-year anniversary of the Declaration of Independence.

Henry Mercer (Henri Mercier) was a Grand Master of the United orders of the American Rite, Strict Observance 1787. In 1853 he Americanized the Thomas Jefferson translation of *The Book of the Holy Grail* for the Chosen peoples, speaking the Chosen language (American English) in the Chosen Land (the United States of America). He was a Patriarch of the Merovingian Gnostic Church, Order of the Holy Grail.

CPSIA information can be obtained
at www.ICGtesting.com
Printed in the USA
LVHW112145300123
738277LV00004B/150

9 781584 451655